Harri Kuisti

Faith is Sanity

© 2025 Harri Kuisti

Kustantaja: BoD · Books on Demand, Mannerheimintie 12 B,

00100 Helsinki, bod@bod.fi

Kirjapaino: Libri Plureos GmbH, Friedensallee 273,

22763 Hampuri, Saksa

ISBN: 978-952-80-9715-0

Be as wise as serpents and as innocent as doves.

Jesus

God is not far from any of us: in him we live, move, and have our being.

Paul

Forword

I admit to being what is known as an Excel Christian, a term coined by a pastor to describe believers who are grounded and wary of fanaticism. I find it difficult to prevent my brain from participating in this venture called faith, and I don't even try.

I am aware that the world does not revolve around me, does not require my ability to understand, and certainly does not wait for my approval as it rushes forward from one incomprehensibility to another.

Even less has the Creator of the Universe built anything on the premise that I, with my fragile brain, would make a philosophical breakthrough behind my desk or even for one fleeting moment grasp something of what is in the mind of the Almighty now, always, and forever.

So, I know my place as a human and the limitations that come with it, but I still believe that God created me in His own image. This means, in my understanding, that I have the right and even the duty to use the thinking ability that I have.

I certainly do not mean that my understanding exceeds even the average human level, let alone that I am particularly intelligent. However, I am wary of the attitude that sometimes appears in all groups of people (not just believers) that requires the acceptance of various viewpoints, perceptions, and beliefs as they are, without critical consideration.

In this book, I have tried to examine various questions, beliefs, and thought patterns that I have encountered as openly as possible, without intending to offend or pressure those who believe in a different way.

I have published most of these short writings earlier in Finnish in a book named "Usko ja järki" (Faith and Intellect). I decided to produce an English translation for two reasons.

First, I have eagerly tried to write comments on some YouTube videos and found it frustrating. One obviously cannot develop the arguments fully in such a short format and what is more, my comments have often been misunderstood or even erased. In this book my thoughts are at least theoretically available to a large audience.

Another reason for the English translation was to try how well the artificial intelligence manages to do the job. In this case I used Copilot. I had previously been impressed by it's performance when translating a text from Finnish to English, and from that further to Swedish, then to German, and so forth through a long chain of European languages I do not understand, and finally back to Finnish.

The final Finnish translation was obviously not the same as the initial text, but the meaning had not changed at all. The language was actually even better and more fluent in the final Finnish version!

I decided to give the AI a chance in translating the book of mine into English. It did a decent job to my Finnish eyes. You are welcome to form your own opinion. I had to do many corrections relying on my own command of English more than on that of an AI tool. I hope I did not change the text to worse formulations.

I write this first chapter on my own because I want to blame the Copilot for some things I have noticed when using it. And I do not wish to have it to read and to translate texts that it may find offensive.

Copilot is definitely "woke" as they say in English. The Finnish language is gender neutral in nature. It is said to be explained by the cold climate: The clothes were the same for both sexes and there were thick layers of them due to the cold climate, so it was not safe to guess if the person was he or she. That is why we have just on word "hän" for both.

The "woke" Copilote had translated the word "hän" to "they" throughout the text, which my English teacher had never accepted.

Just for fun I once tested the political correctness of Copilote by feeding it sentences like "A rich white man gives a Christmas to a poor black child", and invariably it told me: "I am not able to continue this discussion. I wish You can understand that."

But I do not wish to hurt anyone with my texts. So if you find some parts of it offensive (I truly wish you do not) the fault is mine and mine alone. I wish you a good time in reading.

Conciousness

Neuroscientists say that human consciousness and its nature are not yet fully understood. Even those who consider it primarily a phenomenon related to the brain, which cannot exist independently of it, do not try to deny its existence per se. And it would be impossible to deny an obvious fact, even though some people's materialistic worldview drives them to try to explain it purely as a physical, chemical, and biological phenomenon.

The fact that scientists admit that consciousness cannot be fully explained is a very significant point. It strongly challenges the materialistic worldview, as consciousness seems to be something that transcends the boundaries of known sciences. Despite this, materialistically inclined scientists are seem to believe that science will eventually succeed in explaining consciousness in natural scientific terms.

Materialists may also downplay the mystery of consciousness and try to make it appear as just a set of relatively small questions that have not yet been answered: Once science solves those smaller problems, the mystery of consciousness is also hoped to find its scientific explanation.

One attempt to deny the uniqueness of consciousness alongside all the physical events around us is also to refer to everyday sensory experiences, such as smelling the scents of a summer garden, hearing the birds sing, and feeling the boards of a sun-warmed terrace under bare feet.

All those sensations can indeed be explained in scientific terms, but that does not provide any answer to why the person experiencing these things has a strong feeling of a thinking and feeling self, which is aware of its own consciousness, is separate and in some sense independent of the surrounding physical reality, and is able to observe it as if from an outsider's perspective.

A materialist must try to explain these feelings. In the absence of a better theory, it is popular to talk about the illusion of consciousness or self, but upon closer inspection, this is not any kind of explanation of the phenomenon itself. It merely gives known and indisputable observations a new name and attempts to make them sound less relevant.

An illusion is generally understood as a feeling or perception that is not anchored in reality. A materialist scientist believes that only measurement results and the numbers describing them are reality. Since consciousness cannot be measured, it must be classified as an illusion.

This setup also shows how even scientists can resort to circular reasoning in defending their own atheistic and materialistic ideology. It starts from the premise that nothing separate from or outside the physical world exists because there is no convincing evidence for it. And when phenomena are encountered in research that cannot be explained in scientific terms, they are called illusions and claimed not to exist in reality.

It is quite easy for a Christian to explain consciousness as part of the reality created by God. When God is a conscious and feeling person, a human being created in His image is also such. This is anything but a scientific explanation. But how is the idea that everything should be explained scientifically justified? Such a requirement is not self-evident in relation to everything unknown in life, even though it fits well as a starting point for scientific research.

Science has produced a lot of useful knowledge, but that does not mean that there is no reality outside its field of study. Anyone who demands answers to all questions based on scientific experiments and measurements makes science their religion. No one should have to make such a choice, as science and faith do not make each other unnecessary. Both have their own roles.

I think this setup is illustrated by an analogy from the field of music: The harmonica is a fine instrument, and it has its place in music. Still, no one says after a symphony orchestra concert: "It sounded beautiful, but it wasn't based on the use of the harmonica."

When the concept of human consciousness as separate and external to physical reality is accepted, only then is there reason to trust human observations and the conclusions drawn from them. If human consciousness is solely related to brain activity, and that is entirely determined by the laws of physics, the human brain produces thoughts dictated by physical processes, and nothing guarantees that the observations and conclusions made are objectively true.

If it is true that the sensations of consciousness and self are illusions, there is no sure way to know what other delusions our brains might produce. This uncertainty is even greater if it is assumed that human brains have evolved through a long and somewhat random evolutionary process.

Those who oppose the idea that all living things were created through intelligent design, either alongside or instead of evolution, often point out that there are many features in organisms that no one would have intentionally chosen. If all parts of organisms always functioned perfectly, there would be no reason to say so, as a perfect designer could certainly have designed a perfect solution.

It must therefore be concluded that biologists believe there are features in living organisms that are not perfect. If this is true, how do we know that one feature of the brain, the ability to make reliable observations and interpretations, has evolved to perfection over time? There is no reason to trust such a conclusion, especially when the conclusion must be made with the same brains whose functionality the conclusion concerns.

It is true that science relies on extensive collaboration among researchers, and many members of the scientific community check experiments and their interpretations. This is believed to reveal the worst errors in research, but this is not necessarily true if all human brains have the same genetic flaw that prevents reliable thinking. And such a danger is evident because all humans have the same origin.

A worldview that starts from the assumption that human consciousness and the ability to think are gifts from the Creator is more logical and does not contain logical contradictions. Only from this basis can one expect research to produce reliable information. This worldview cannot be proven to be correct, but if it is not true, it is impossible to prove anything. A materialistic worldview would leave us at the mercy of our illusions.

Free will

People often feel that they have at least some control over small decisions in their lives. Based on their own experiences, they can freely decide whether to raise their right or left hand or perhaps put both hands in their pockets.

However, common sense suggests that people often cannot freely choose their profession, for example. Many study places usually have more applicants than can be accepted. After graduating, they also cannot freely decide which company or other organization to work for, as many people and chance play a role in how well the job seeker's wishes come true.

Most people feel that all life's decision-making situations roughly fall into these two categories. Additionally, there are many things that a person cannot choose at all. For example, the country and family into which each person is born are naturally beyond human decision-making power.

This is all self-evident to many based on their own experiences, but especially philosophers and scientists have long been interested in the extent to which humans are truly free to make choices. In this context, it is essential to define what is meant by free will. Some understand free will ideally as unlimited and reject the whole concept because no individual's freedom to choose can ever be complete. It is clear that an individual's decisions often affect other people, and one person's unlimited decision-making power could not exist without restricting the freedom of others.

Some deniers of the existence of free will believe that human choices are purely determined by the laws of nature, as the starting point is to see humans only as complex biological machines. According to proponents of this view, humans have no self, soul, or consciousness independent of the body.

The materialistic view of humanity described above can also be said to be the basis for interpretations made from research results on the subject. For example, activities in the human brain related to decisions have been observed even before a person becomes aware of their own choice. Some have seen this as evidence that the decision begins as a physical activity in the brain guided by the laws of nature and is beyond the reach of consciously made human choices.

When such far-reaching conclusions are drawn about the time difference between the physical activity of the brain and the experience of conscious choice, it is reasonable to ask how someone can be sure of the correctness of their chosen starting point.

Only if human thinking is considered purely physical brain activity can something be concluded about the relationship between the physical activity of the brain and conscious choice. However, this starting point has not been proven and is unlikely to be proven correct.

If, on the other hand, conscious and unconscious human thinking and decisions are seen as at least partially independent of the physical activity of the brain, it cannot be ruled out that the unconscious decision of a person may have been the trigger for the entire sequence of events: In this way of thinking, the unconscious decision of the human mind may have preceded the physically observable brain activity and the subsequent phase in which the person becomes aware of the decision they have made.

Possibly, the order could be always the same in all human consciousness: First, an unconscious impulse independent of physical brain activity arises, which then triggers physically observable activity in the brain before the thought is consciously recognized.

This is naturally pure speculation, intended only to provide an example of a non-materialistic interpretation. An opponent of the concept of free will cannot dismiss the existence of such a remote possibility except by arguing that in their worldview, physical reality is always dominant, and therefore humans cannot have free will.

Thus, if it is claimed that the concept of free will is in conflict with experimental results, this is based on failure to think logically. It is only in conflict with one possible interpretation of the results, which is based on the assumption of the dominance of physical reality. Starting from this one and the same premise, one arrives at an interpretation of the experimental results that considers the experiment to prove the premise correct. This is circular reasoning.

The claim that human free will does not exist is self-defeating. Since the strong experience of free will in humans cannot be denied, it has been labeled an illusion. This may seem like a plausible explanation at first, but upon closer inspection, it undermines all objective thinking.

If humans are considered susceptible to such a fundamental illusion as that of free will, then what is the basis for believing that humans can think and understand anything else correctly?

All attempts to prove the reliable functioning of the brain require careful thought and take the reliability of the brain as a starting point. This again leads to circular reasoning.

Why, then, do some oppose the idea of free will? There can be many reasons. I suspect that the most common reason given is the desire to defend the truth, even though individuals themselves feel that their will is free. It is said that the truth proclaimed by science must be accepted even when it seems contrary to common sense.

Those who deny free will, presenting themselves as defenders of truth, ignore the truth I have presented: Reliable conclusions require reliable brains.

Although declaring the experience of free will an illusion seems very important to many people, they still act as if their own will is free and as if their listeners and readers can decide how they respond to the message of these proclaimers.

Deniers of free will thus act contrary to their proclamation and do not seem to believe it themselves. But a materialistic worldview requires the denial of free will, even if this leads to a philosophical dead end.

Humans have the ability to use their intellect as they wish, even when they use it to deny the existence of this freedom. The more intelligent a person is, the easier it is for them to find arguments for or against any claim.

On the other hand, the idea that human will is not entirely free gets support from an unexpected direction: Christianity. A materialist is not pleased with this, as the denial of free will was supposed to support the idea that human actions are determined by the laws of nature.

The Bible presents the idea in many places that the whole world is under the power of evil, which can be assumed to mean that the human will cannot be completely free. Paul describes this with the following words in his letter to the Romans: "I do not do the good I want to do, but the evil I do not want to do."

Paul thus suggests that actions of people are not always guided by their own will, but by the sin that dwells within them. Thinking is part of human action, and it is possible that deniers of free will are partly right in this and that their thinking is guided by the forces of evil.

The existence of evil is a possible explanation for why some proclaim a message they do not seem to believe themselves. Such an explanation is logical and internally consistent, but it does not support a materialistic worldview.

A person can also surrender his will to God's guidance and say, like Jesus: "Let your will be done, not mine." This can be thought to lead to God Himself using His power for the person's benefit and changing the circumstances to make it easier for the person to act correctly.

Such surrender to God's guidance does not happen without the person's own consent and does not, in that sense, remove the person's free will. Similarly, rejecting God also requires a choice from the person. In this setup, there may be a hidden motive to oppose the idea of the reality of free will.

When a person is under the guidance of evil, and his will is restricted in this sense, the apparent interest of this evil is to keep the person in the belief that no conscious choice away from this setup is possible.

A person may also find the idea comforting that he does not have the freedom to choose otherwise and that he is shaped by circumstances and the laws of nature.

The core message of the Bible is that a person has the opportunity to choose which supernatural entity to ally with. Turning to God requires that the person does so of his own free will. God does not come into anyone's life by force.

God's opponent does not require the person to ask for help or even believe in his existence. The final outcome for the person will be the same, even if the person maintains his materialistic belief until the end of his life.

A person must choose for himself whether to jump into the stream of evil, even if he does not believe it to be real. From the perspective of the evil side, it is enough for a person to reject his Creator. After that, he is offered many different canoes, boats, and barrels to descend the rapids of their life towards the final waterfall.

If a person understands that his life is rushing towards destruction, he can at any time before plunging into the waterfall, reach out his hand upwards and ask for help from the highest authority in the universe and do that out of his own free will and be saved from eternal separation from God.

Is atheism based on science?

I do not know much about philosophy, psychology, sociology, or other sciences, but I know that people's perceptions have been continuously changing as their knowledge has increased. I also know that people have always had many beliefs that have later proven to be wrong.

As past beliefs have often been revealed to be incorrect when things have been studied using scientific methods, many have begun to consider modern perceptions as fundamentally correct, even though a more justified approach would be to assume that future scientific research will reveal also current perceptions to be inaccurate, if not entirely wrong.

I have heard many scientists say that doing science is a process in which theories are constantly corrected as more information is obtained. I thus assume that many scientists have a suitably humble attitude towards what they know or what can generally be known.

Those who work with science are only human and cannot help that we do not know everything. Atheists often accuse adherents of various religions of trying to fill gaps in knowledge with blind faith, but in my view, this is common to all people and adherents of all ideologies.

A person must take certain things as starting points on which they build their worldview. One possible choice is to assume that everything has an explanation in this world, even if it has not yet been found. This is a meaningful starting point for scientific work, but one that cannot be proven correct.

When we take as a starting point that no factors outside the natural world affect the phenomena we observe, this must be acknowledged as a basic assumption, not claimed to be proven by research results. If one tries to prove the initial assumption correct with the resulting research findings, it is circular reasoning, as I have noted previously.

It is only possible to say, based on research results, that this or that phenomenon can be explained without resorting to supernatural causes, but that does not mean that supernatural things could not exist. Natural sciences cannot provide any information about supernatural factors.

If a natural scientist makes statements about supernatural things, it cannot be based on scientific research. It is a matter of philosophical private thinking, opinions, or personal beliefs.

Science could not make progress if knowledge was not allowed to accumulate, but each new generation should repeat the experiments of the past, to be sure of the facts by checking them again. The reliability of previous research must be assumed.

An individual is in an even more difficult position in this respect, as he must take most of the ever-expanding mass of knowledge as given and build their own thinking on it. They cannot personally investigate everything and repeat the experiments of others. They must decide to believe what the scientific community considers to have already proven correct, even though the same scientists admit that it is only the best attempt so far to provide a natural explanation for a phenomenon.

It can be said that every belief that cannot be proven true is based on faith, although scientists prefer to use other terms for such as premise, paradigm, or theoretical framework.

Everyone has the right to use the words they prefer to describe the fact that not everything can be known and that some beliefs must be assumed to be true as the basis for research, even if they cannot be proven right. But anyone who claims not to believe in anything but simply knows everything worth knowing is either intellectually dishonest or does not understand the difference between knowing and believing.

Atheists often view those who believe in God as if they resort to their faith only to understand otherwise incomprehensible things in our visible world. This is a misconception, as faith is about much greater things.

I do not even try to describe what faith can mean to different people, but I focus here on emphasizing how faith in God affects thinking. Not all believers claim that God is behind all currently unexplained observations. Most believers I know primarily seek natural and everyday explanations for natural events.

The effort to find natural explanations for the phenomena of the world can be called a naturalistic approach. For a believer, naturalism can be a tool for thinking, while for an atheist, it is an all-encompassing philosophical approach.

It is one thing to claim that many things can be explained naturally without resorting to factors outside the visible world, and quite another to declare that there is nothing outside the natural world.

There is no neutral and indisputably objective overall view of the universe, although atheism or naturalism is often presented as such. There are roughly only two options: Either there is nothing outside the observable universe, or there is (or may be) something. Neither of these approaches can be proven right or wrong.

I have only mentioned agnosticism in parentheses, although it differs from belief in God by claiming that there is no knowledge of God's existence. From the atheist's point of view, agnosticism can be seen as opposed to atheism, as the atheist believes they know that God does not exist or cannot exist.

In his excellent book "Warranted Christian Belief," philosopher Alvin Plantinga demonstrates the internal contradiction of the claim that there can be no knowledge of God: If there can be no knowledge about this person at all, then how can it be claimed that there is knowledge about one of this person's attributes (existence)?

Plantinga also presents a thought experiment: If there were a God, such a person could, if they wished, express themselves in a manner of their choosing to those people they want to know that they exist. Therefore, if there were a God, belief in him would not necessarily be blind but could also be justified.

Plantinga's thought experiment is not proof of God's existence, but it is an indication that it might be possible to know something about God if he exists. The actual question, whether God exists, does not get any answer through this thought experiment.

Why do people choose such different ways to approach the question of God's existence? There can be many reasons. One is the moral consequences of the answer: If one believes that God exists, it is natural to also believe that God might have expectations or demands regarding a person's life or lifestyle. Therefore, the question is not trivial but one that involves values and moral concepts.

Some atheists may reject the idea of God simply as uncomfortable, while those who choose the attitude of faith may believe for moral reasons or believe just in case.

A person may also believe because faith provides comfort and security. An atheist might scoff at such an attitude and see it as a sign of weakness, but it must be remembered that belief in the existence of God has been quite common for millennia and dos not seem to be disappear from the world any time soon.

So, if one believes that God does not exist, but that everything came about by chance and humans are the result of an evolutionary process, one still cannot deny that many people believe in God. From an evolutionary perspective, belief in God must, on the contrary, be a beneficial trait for the success and survival of the human species.

Therefore, I can justifiably say that I believe in God also because evolution has given me faith, because this is a favorable trait.

A person can also believe or not believe based on what his admired role models advise him to do. This selection criterion naturally does not help in finding an indisputable answer. How far the answer can deviate from reality most likely depends on the reliability of the mentioned role models.

Human reliability is never certain, and it is even more uncertain when people have deeply personal reasons to commit to a certain way of believing.

Ideally, each person carefully weighs various facts and chooses the option that best explains the observed facts. Even then, however, it is only a matter of choosing the most credible option, not knowing for sure which one is the absolutely correct choice.

One essential difference can be identified between atheism and belief in God: If I believe in God, I will never know that I was wrong, but if I am right, I may very well know in the future that I chose correctly. If I decide not to believe in God, I will never know that I was right, but I may very well be held accountable for my wrong choice.

If God exists, why then does He make it so difficult to be sure of His existence? I answer that no one can reasonably claim that God has not done everything possible to make people believe in Him voluntarily. God, if He exists, could, if He wished, make His existence so indisputable that no one could choose not to believe. In that case, a person would not even have any faith, but objective and certain knowledge of the matter.

Since I tend to make choices that feel right for me, whether to believe or not, how can I know that I have been completely honest with myself? Perhaps it is as the apostle Paul wrote: God's existence is fundamentally a self-evident fact to all humans, but they still have the freedom to reject this knowledge.

The essential difference between humans and a possibly existing God is that humans know they do not know everything. If God exists, he knows everything. Therefore, humans have no competence or authority to define how God should act. Humans only have the freedom to choose whether to believe or not.

Dishonest question

Militant atheists often tend to use the so-called straw man method when arguing against the existence of God. The most childish of these methods is probably comparing the Creator of the Universe to Santa Claus. For example, one of the most well-known atheists has stated that he is "agnostic" about the existence of Santa Claus.

Humor is sometimes used as a way to divert the audience's thoughts away from the poor foundations of one's own views. It often also aims to ridicule those who think differently and make them appear foolish and gullible.

Most atheists, of course, understand that comparing God to Santa Claus is a category error. Firstly, except for very young children, hardly anyone seriously believes in Santa Claus; the character is known to be fictional and intended as such.

In contrast, a large portion of the world's population believes in some form of higher power or person. They form a very diverse group representing various nationalities, social statuses, professions, and intelligence levels. It cannot be reasonably argued that all these people are more easily misled or naively gullible than others.

Another example of the use of the straw man tactic is to claim that people believe only in a "God of the gaps." This often refers to the primitive myths of ancient people, which were created before modern science provided physical and other natural explanations for the observations of the real world's astonishing phenomena, such as thunder.

The truth is that scientific insights have indeed made many of the old misconceptions outdated or inaccurate.

However, these misconceptions cannot be said to have been solely religious; often, it was simply a matter of lack of knowledge. An example of such a misunderstanding from the past is the idea that swallows spend the winter in the mud at the bottom of lakes. This idea likely arose from the observation that swallows were often seen searching for insects at lower altitudes, such as near the surface of lakes, during the cooler weather of late summer.

We now know that swallows migrate to warmer regions for the winter, and we are convinced that electrical phenomena provide a good explanation for thunder. However, modern science often presents a series of increasingly difficult questions with each new discovery.

Cosmologists have suggested that not all phenomena observed in space can be explained without resorting to the concepts of dark matter and dark energy. According to some estimates, most of the matter and energy in the entire universe may belong to these so-called dark categories.

Physicists, however, are currently unable to explain the composition of dark matter or the properties of dark energy. In addition, even the better-known ordinary forms of matter and energy still hide many mysteries, and it can be argued that the natural sciences have cleared an ever larger space for the "God of the gaps."

Humans have always been troubled by questions deeper than the mud at the bottom of lakes and puzzled by mysteries greater than the cosmos. These questions can never be answered by science, because science only studies what can be factually known.

Scientists sometimes characterize their own opinions as arising from science, but in terms of scientific work, their private thoughts have as little significance as their favorite colors or their grandmothers' collected cake recipes.

However, private opinions have often been seen to find their way into the speeches of scientists. This probably often happens simply because science is ultimately done by otherwise ordinary people who are just driven by a greater than usual interest in their own field.

I do not claim to be a philosopher, but many scientists who have turned into atheist activists do not seem willing to engage in deep and critical reflection on the foundations of scientific work. This can be inferred at least from their tendency to lock their philosophical positions rather lightly, consciously or unconsciously applying the aforementioned straw man method.

I do not take an absolute stance on whether conscious or unconscious errors in thinking are worse for a scientist, but since I do not believe in the fundamental goodness of people, I assume that at least some militant atheists aim to convert others to their side by any means necessary, and intellectual dishonesty is part of their toolkit.

Intellectual dishonesty is evident, for example, when atheists pose a question for which they have already predetermined the only acceptable answer. The question is: How do you prove the existence of God, and why should anyone believe in it?

On the surface, these questions may seem sincere, but it soon becomes clear that they are not. It quickly becomes apparent that the questioner means something entirely

different by "God" than, for example, a Christian respond-
ent.

The atheist has already defined God in their mind as a
small straw man, a god of the gaps, that most Christians
do not believe in and do not want to defend. But the atheist goes even further: They pose a question whose correct
answer they, as humans, could not even understand.

And the atheists does what no one should ever do: They
set their own understanding as the highest authority in the
universe and declare everything they cannot comprehend
as pure imagination.

When I think about the nature of God, the idea of the
Creator of everything comes to mind. A person who is outside of all physical reality and the universe he created, as
well as time, but still, it is his reality and his cosmos, and
he is in it in some sense always present, or rather, the universe is within them.

God is incomprehensible to a Christian, but non-exist-
ent to an atheist, as the latter accepts only such elements
in their reality that they imagine they can understand. The
Christian, on the other hand, starts from the premise that
God is great and beyond human understanding.

The atheist first creates a ridiculous straw man that he
believes the Christian worships. And although creating a
straw man is a cheap debate tactic and reflects an unwill-
ingness to genuinely understand the opponent's opinion
or way of thinking, the atheist may not see himself as doing anything wrong in this regard, as he believes that all
gods anyway are created by humans themselves.

A Christian may not feel he can intellectually prove God's existence to anyone, but they might bravely try to paint a picture of the greatest force and person in the universe and the ultimate and original Creator of everything. This message goes over the atheist's head because they demand the defense of the straw man and do not want to accept anyone above themselves.

I once heard about blind children who were promised a visit to a farm to meet real cows, sheep, and horses. They were used to playing only with small plastic toy animals that fit in their hands. Upon arrival, some of the children immediately crouched down, reaching out to find the "real" animals they were supposed to meet.

Some atheists are so accustomed to crafting dolls named God that they direct their search downward and crouch toward a small god. They proclaim that they do not need God, sever the doll's head, and believe they have defended atheism exemplarily.

The truth is that no one needs straw dolls. A Christian justifiably discards such a thing, strives toward the real God, and believes he will meet Him after this life.

An atheist recognizes only straw dolls, keeps them as memories of defeated and destroyed gods, and declares that he does not need anything he does not understand. An atheist is like a boat floating on the open sea that does not need water for anything, or like a compass needle that pretends it does not feel the magnetic field, claiming that the misguided compasses themselves have created a magnetic field in their imagination in order to get some direction and purpose.

Salvation plan

God planned everything. I could start and end this chapter with that one statement, but I will still try to describe the events and settings in more detail. Behind everything is still the one and the same Almighty, who has made a whole series of moves throughout human history to reach goals beyond human understanding.

The process initiated by the Creator long ago is still ongoing, as new people are constantly being born into this anything but finished world, who at least at the peak moments of their self-reflection know they are imperfect.

Imperfection is precisely the human condition. Only in moments of complete foolishness can someone fail to see his own shortcomings, and only a 2-year-old might consider himself omnipotent.

I do not believe that humans will ever become perfect, as God is perfect, omnipotent, and omniscient, because the Creator has not intended for humans to ever become God. Such an outcome would be completely absurd and impossible to achieve. Such cannot be the content of God's salvation plan.

Why then can't humans become God? This question is absurd when considering what God is like. Various attributes can be associated with God in human thinking, and one of them is that He has always been the same and never changes.

No-one or nothing can become God, for then at least this one change would have occurred. Therefore, one does not become God, nor is one born as such, for He has always existed. But a human being has come into existence at a specific moment and was born months later on a precisely known day and within a few hours.

A human being is born and changes all the time thereafter. This is evident to everyone, but the most essential thing is what a human being changes into. The Almighty devised the salvation plan precisely to manage this process of change, not to create beings that compete with Him and, against better knowledge, imagine themselves to be gods.

The Creator could, of course, have made humans believe they have always existed, but such gods would not be omniscient, as they would not even know the truth about themselves.

I believe that a human being can become perfect in only one sense: They can become fully human. What does that mean? To me, it means that they know and acknowledge the truth about themselves: They exist only because God created them, and they are entirely dependent on their Creator.

In the beginning of the Bible, it is told about the creation of the world and how everything was initially perfect. As a child, I didn't even think about it in more detail, but I had the impression that the world was created in a week, and the first human couple fell into sin no later than the second week. However, the world and humans maybe remained perfect for a long time, even though the total collapse is told about already in the third chapter of the Bible.

It is not essential how long a period the first three chapters of the Bible cover. The key is to know that a great catastrophe happened in the third chapter, and the rest of the Bible tells how the mess created is cleaned up and how the aftermath is dealt with.

In other words, the first three chapters of the Bible justify why humans and the world need to be saved, and then it is explained how that is done.

At this point, an Excel Christian must ask: Didn't the all-knowing God foresee how dangerous it was to give humans the freedom of choice? Didn't He know that humans would make a wrong choice?

Even people know that soon after a newly built bridge is completed, a group of men with fishing rods will crowd behind the railings, despite a sign prohibiting fishing. The Creator must have known that the prohibition to eat the fruit of one specific tree made that particular tree interesting.

I can imagine with my mind's eye how Adam and Eve first circled the tree from a distance, but gradually some inexplicable force made them walk closer and later circle around it daily. Possibly, over time, their bare feet wore a path around the tree before Eve finally reached out and took the fruit.

Did God not know what was going to happen? There can be at least two answers to this, depending on which aspect of perfection one places more weight on. One can first think that the perfectly omniscient God foresaw the impending catastrophe. Alternatively, it is possible that the Creator succeeded so perfectly in His endeavor to create free will for humans that even He could not be certain of the outcome.

I find the latter option more credible, as it was entirely possible for God to create humans as He wished. If He had seen that a human created in a certain way would choose wrongly with 100% certainty, He would have practically forced the human to fall into sin if He had made the human that way.

I think that God created humans to choose freely and therefore could not be sure of what humans would do. The situation is similar to when a man sends a love letter to a woman and cannot know how she will respond. The man wants the woman to respond favorably of her own free will. If he is a millionaire, he does not want the woman to choose him just for that reason. The man wants the woman to love him even if he is penniless. If he were a mentalist or hypnotist, he would not want to manipulate the woman into loving him. The man wants to be chosen by the woman when she is completely free in her choice.

The all-knowing God, who exists outside of time, may see all the outcomes of free choices and their combinations simultaneously and acts for the benefit of the person He loves in all of them, in ways that help the person but do not restrict his freedom of choice.

It is possible that in God's timeless reality, there is a branch of the tree of free choices where Adam and Eve, with their children, live happily forever and choose rightly time and again, never falling into sin. I know that I do not live on such a branch of branching reality, and such a world is not mine.

I live in my own reality, and billions of people share this same experience. If there is an infinite number of parallel realities based on different free choices, they are reality for God, not for me or any other inhabitants of this planet. A human can never know how God, who lives outside of time, sees events after making humans completely free to act as they wish every second, minute, and hour.

The salvation plan I write about here relates to the reality we are in now. The central aspect of Christianity was what Jesus did 2000 years ago: He sacrificed Himself to fix what Adam and Eve and all their descendants had broken and continue to break.

However, a few things are difficult for me to understand. Firstly: why was a sacrifice needed at all? Couldn't the Almighty have just forgiven? Sometimes the answer given is that God is holy and His nature demands punishment for the guilty: In a just universe, actions must have consequences.

It can also be thought that the evil deeds committed by humans start chain reactions that must be stopped with sufficiently big good deeds. I assume that the sum of the evil deeds committed by humans of their own free will is so great that the death of the Son of God was needed. The alternative might have been the death of all the people on the planet: Sinning stops when the last human is removed from the stage.

But God had already tested that option by allowing the flood to drown most peole. After the flood, however, people had continued to do evil of their own free will, so God next tried to see if clear prohibitions and commands would help people refrain from doing more evil: God gave His law to Israel through Moses. That experiment also failed miserably, and people learned to follow the law formally and superficially, and those who had previously openly done evil soon became secret sinners and hypocrites.

But possibly hypocrisy could be curbed if secret sins were revealed. In this hope, the Almighty made some people prophets and tasked them with exposing the secret evil deeds of others and threatening them with punishment. That didn't help either, and eventually, God had to carry out His threats and allow other nations to forcibly take a large portion of the Israelites away from their own land.

In exile, some Israelites repented of their evil deeds, and eventually, God restored them to their own land. However, people had not permanently changed, and their wickedness gradually began to flourish again.

When God saw that nothing else helped, He sent His own Son into the midst of Israel in the most cunning undercover operation in world history. Officially, Jesus tried to appeal to the Israelites and bring them back to God. However, the real purpose was to get people to kill the Son of God.

Lucifer is not an equal opponent to God and, for example, is not omniscient. Therefore, he could not read the situation well enough and thought he could best disrupt God's plan by inciting people to kill Jesus before He could win them over with His miracles and wise teachings.

I assume the Devil congratulated himself when he saw the Nazarene hanging on the cross and laughed triumphantly when Jesus took His last breath. He did not anticipate the short-lived nature of his victory and likely fell into a fit of powerless rage when Jesus unexpectedly rose from the dead.

From Lucifer's perspective, the worst possible outcome was that the death and resurrection of the Son of God had two astonishing consequences: Firstly, God declared that the death of the Son of God was sufficient to atone for the sins of all people (past, present, and future, even those yet to be born). Lucifer boiled with rage upon realizing that he could no longer justifiably accuse people of their sins or tempt them to give up and stop trying to follow God's will.

The second surprising effect was seen on the first Pentecost, when something strange had happened to people: Notably, there was an increased courage among people to share God's salvation plan with others. Many were ready to spread the message even at the risk of their lives. The devil soon noticed that Christianity spread most effectively when believers were persecuted, but he still could not help his nature. He continues to try to get many to oppose Jesus' followers by all means, but there are still more Christians in the world, both proportionally and in absolute numbers, than ever before.

The implementation of the plan is still ongoing, but everyone has the opportunity to participate in it in his own way and receive salvation by silently saying in their mind: "Jesus, forgive my sins." If a person doubts the whole story, they can just pray: "Jesus, if you exist, help me." It works.

Miracles

In everyday language, miracles can refer to anything surprising and generally favorable from a human perspective, such as a poorly prepared student passing an exam with a good grade or getting a trip to the Canary Islands at an unexpectedly low price. Defined this way, a miracle can be said to be almost synonymous with good luck.

However, more narrowly defined, a miracle can be said to involve a factor outside the reality perceived by our senses, even if the event is sometimes largely explained by completely ordinary things.

The store of natural explanations for humans has grown with the increase in scientific knowledge. Thus, there is nothing miraculous about a thunderstorm for modern humans, nor if a lightning bolt happens to strike the lightning rod of a high hospital building. However, if one of the hospital's patients were to recover when the lightning struck the building, it might seem like a miracle to the person himself, but others would likely seek natural explanations and, if necessary, appeal to coincidence.

The recovery of two or three seriously ill patients as a result of a lightning strike might already seem difficult to explain naturally, not to mention if half of the patients in a large hospital suddenly recovered, including a few who were in coma. How dramatic an event each person requires to admit that it is a miracle depends on the individual.

Fundamentally, no one ever needs to admit that a miracle has occurred unless they happen to witness one. The simplest natural explanation is that eyewitness accounts are the result of misunderstandings, exaggerations, or even outright falsehoods.

Eyewitness accounts, photographs, and videos have long lost their value as evidence, especially in the media and social media, where many parties are known to have an interest in influencing people's opinions and behavior or simply shocking them.

I myself approach all non-Biblical accounts of miracles with caution precisely because of their unreliability. This is despite the fact that I believe in the possibility of miracles in principle: I believe that many astonishing things have indeed happened.

Jesus rising from the dead was probably the greatest miracle in history. I believe in it. So why do I trust ancient eyewitness accounts when I am skeptical of much more recent reports? Isn't there a risk that the stories have become more exaggerated over time?

The historicity of Jesus' resurrection has been extensively studied, and many more qualified than I have concluded that the evidence related to it is reliable, but that is not the only reason I believe in it.

The main reason to believe, in my opinion, is simple: All beliefs related to Jesus were highly controversial, and he and his followers had many opponents. This can be inferred from the fact that he was killed. This is an indisputable fact, and I have not heard anyone who has studied the subject question the crucifixion itself.

When Jesus' supporters began to publicly claim that he had risen from the dead, it would have been very simple for the opponents to prove these claims false by opening the tomb and showing Jesus' body.

Of course, it was not appropriate for those who followed Jewish law to examine the body closely or touch it. But it would have been easy to show that the tomb was not empty. Why didn't Jesus' opponents resort to such an obvious means to silence the talk of resurrection?

Jesus had already been seen as a political threat by the Jewish leaders during his lifetime, and his followers were worsening the situation by claiming he had risen from the dead. They had every reason to prove that the resurrection was a lie, so why didn't they open the tomb publicly and then arrest those spreading false information? The answer is simple: They already knew the tomb was empty.

Since the tomb was undeniably empty, Jesus' opponents had only one option left: They had to come up with a story that Jesus' body had been stolen.

It would have been possible for Jesus' followers to have taken his body, hidden it, and then convinced everyone else that he had risen from the dead. However, this is a very unlikely explanation for what happened. They must have firmly believed in Jesus' resurrection, as many of them were willing to pay with their lives for spreading this claim.

We know that many people throughout history have been willing to die for various ideologies and beliefs, so such an attitude does not yet guarantee the accuracy of the belief. But no one who had stolen their teacher's body would have been able to believe in the resurrection themselves and would not have been willing to die for their lie.

Could it then be possible that some of Jesus' close circle had stolen the body and lied to everyone else? Even in that explanation, there are at least two problems: Firstly, they were most obviously disappointed that the miracle-working Messiah had turned out to be a weak ordinary person who allowed himself to be killed in a shameful manner. Why would they have tried to save their Savior's reputation and honor at the cost of their lives?

On the other hand, Jesus was claimed to have appeared to many simultaneously. Someone would have had to convincingly present Jesus in front of those who had closely followed their teacher's every word and gesture for years, which would have been a hard thing to do. In conclusion, the theory that Jesus' body was stolen simply does not seem credible.

I have come to believe that the most credible explanation is that a genuine miracle occurred: In my view, Jesus truly rose from the dead. I really believe in the greatest miracle of all time.

On the other hand, it should also be noted that sometimes believers tend to exaggerate events by claiming, for example, that they have received a certificate of healing from a doctor. However, these are rarely, if ever, presented in public. I believe such a claim should not be made at all without simultaneously showing the listeners the doctor's certificate, if one exists.

It is questionable to accuse those demanding evidence of unbelief if, at the same time, one appeals to a secular authority, such as a doctor's statement. And if the alleged doctor's certificate does not actually exist, one is also guilty of lying.

Some believers also tend to see miracles where there are none. For example, it may be said that an item was left on a park bench due to carelessness. It cannot be called a miracle if a forgetful person returns a minute later and finds his wallet where he left it.

If opportunity makes a thief, a person who forgets items behind unintentionally sets traps for his neighbors and exposes their immortal souls to the danger of eternal damnation. Such a person should, following a modified version of the Lord's Prayer, ask not to lead others into temptation.

Different denominations have varying attitudes towards the possibility of miracles. Charismatic Christians may accept an event as a miracle without much investigation. The most common healing miracle is probably one leg suddenly growing to the same length as the other when the person has actually just corrected their back posture. It is also claimed that the Creator of the Universe has diligently cured colds, while unbelievers may have to sneeze for an extra day in the worst case.

When I visited Rome, I noticed how typical it has been for Mary to appear to nobles whose funds were needed for church construction. As I understand it, the Catholic Church generally carefully investigates events before starting to talk about miracles, but how can one prevent unholy deals where everyone wins except the truth? A priest who investigates a noble's story of Mary's apparition declares the miracle genuine, gets the money for the church, and quietly sanctifies the marriage of the noble who has just impregnated his maid.

My intention is not to criticize any denomination or religion, but I believe that everyone has the right to choose what they believe in. Practically, everyone also has to make a choice about what they believe and what they do not, as no one can verify all the knowledge related to the universe himself. It is also not possible to know what exists outside the physical universe, or if there is anything at all, at least not just by examining what can be perceived with the senses.

Rubik's cube and the creation of life

If we disregard the fact that the Rubik's Cube is a racist toy where the goal is to get different colors to their own areas, it is an extremely fascinating puzzle. In a standard Rubik's Cube, there are 6 center pieces, 8 corner pieces, and 12 edge pieces, making a total of only 26 pieces. Yet, the pieces of the cube can be arranged in 43,252,003,274,489,856,000 different ways. The number roughly has 18 zeros after the number 43!

Despite the vast number of possible arrangements, the cube is always at most 20 moves away from its solved state. This may seem impossible to believe for someone who has ever played with the cube. Probably no human can see the necessary moves just by looking at a scrambled cube. Presumably, only God can do that. For this reason, the number 20 is referred to as God's number.

However, people can solve the Rubik's Cube in just a few seconds after learning a systematic way to twist it. These methods require a person to recognize certain positions or patterns of the cube and memorize sequences of moves that transition the cube from one state to another. By doing so, the cube can be solved through certain predefined intermediate steps. Even the fastest people in the world have to make about 60 moves to solve the cube.

The Rubik's Cube is quite simple, yet impossible to solve just by randomly twisting it without any system. It also cannot be solved by looking at just a few pieces at a time: The solver must have the current overall state of the cube in mind and an understanding of the state the cube needs to be in at each stage of the solution.

No one believes that the Rubik's Cube can be solved just by randomly twisting it, nor do its pieces move to the correct positions even if it accidentally ends up spinning in the washing machine with the laundry.

It would also be very difficult for a person to systematically try all possible sequences of moves to get the cube into the desired order. Even if someone could endure the monotonous task of trying different sequences of moves, a human lifetime would not be nearly enough, as it would take over 100 billion years to go through all possible arrangements of the Rubik's Cube at a rate of 10 moves per second.

But as mentioned, the fastest people can solve the cube in a few seconds, but they have the overall state of the cube in mind and know how to solve it.

It is clear that the Rubik's Cube is very simple compared to a living cell, let alone entire organisms. I am not qualified to present numerical values related to biology that could be meaningfully compared to the complexity of solving the Rubik's Cube. However, it is obvious to me that a human or an animal is vastly more complex than the mentioned plastic toy, and there can be no disagreement about this.

Despite the fact that many top experts in biology consider chance the best explanation for the origin of life, I find it impossible to believe in this theory. Even a simple plastic puzzle does not solve itself by chance; the person twisting it must know what he is doing.

The idea that the incomprehensible complexity of life could have arisen by chance without some form of intelligent guidance is impossible for me to accept, even if there is a mechanism called natural selection that destroys bad experiments and allows the best to continue.

I can understand that some organisms survive better in competition than others, but that does not yet explain what or who brought a whole bunch of ready-made and complex entities into the competition. I cannot believe in chance's ability to create these functional alternatives.

I know that one eye structure works better than another, but an eye that can see in any way is inevitably very complex. A hypothetical and simple precursor to the eye that does not produce vision cannot provide any competitive advantage over other blind organisms, and therefore cannot evolve into anything better through natural selection.

So how did the first functional eye originate? I cannot believe it came about by chance, even if some evolutionary biologist tries to convince me otherwise. The same problem likely applies to other organs, even individual cells, but the claim that the eye originated by chance is the hardest for me to accept.

I know, a hypothesis has been presented that first a structure appeared that was not an eye but just a thing that was somewhat sensitive to light. The researchers have developed such speculations further and shown how the thing could have gradually evolved into an actual eye. But I still find it hard to believe in such a miraculous process happening by chance even if each step forward could in theory have given some advantage in competition.

I do not accept these theories because they just do not sound credible. The overall complexity of an eye is so big that it is not feasible that it could be explained by evolution. It is much easier to believe that different versions of an eye could emerge through such a process.

One has to bear in mind that there is no evidence that such thing has ever happened: It has not been proved that a fully functional eye has been produced by evolution. It is just the only possibility from the materialistic point of view but accepting such a theory requires much faith. For me it is much easier to believe in a Creator.

Those who know more than I have said that also the survival of life requires accurately right conditions. Our planet's diameter is thousands of kilometers, but life is found only within a few tens of kilometers from sea level.

Although bacteria and viruses are said to be found even within permafrost and deep beneath the Earth's surface, the survival of life is not guaranteed if conditions change too much or too quickly. This has been particularly noted by scientists concerned about the habitability of our planet.

It is said that even the constants of nature must have suitable values for life to be possible. In countries where winters are cold, it is important that ice is lighter than liquid water. Otherwise, the thousands of lakes in my country (Finland) would freeze from bottom to top during winters, and fish could not live in them. Many crucial properties of water and other substances depend on natural constants. Why are their values favorable for life?

The Rubik's Cube is a simple toy compared to life, but it cannot be solved without an overall understanding, just by looking at individual pieces or by relying on chance. Creating the much more complex thing called life has required even more that the Creator knew what he was doing.

Israel

I acknowledge that the decades-long conflict between Israel and its neighbors is an extremely complex issue and cannot be resolved in any simple way. I am writing primarily from one perspective: The Jewish state has a moral right to exist.

I remind my readers that it is permissible to criticize all people when they commit injustices. Therefore, it is acceptable to criticize the policies of the current state of Israel without deserving to be labeled as anti-Semitic. Similarly, terrorism practiced in the Middle East should be condemned without being accused of Islamophobia.

I believe that no country divides opinions as sharply as Israel. Many people seem to have a tendency to demand more from the Jewish state than from any other country. There are many reasons for this.

It is often pointed out that Israel is the only democracy in the Middle East and must act according to its ideals. Its neighboring countries are not held to the same standard because they do not represent Western values in any way. This is as unfair as demanding exemplary behavior from the best students in a class while allowing the poorly behaved students to continue in their usual manner.

Another example of using two different standards would be to leave a serial killer unpunished for a traffic violation or theft and to imprison an otherwise exemplary citizen without a trial for committing these offenses.

It should not be possible to lower the standards of moral requirements and avoid criticism directed at those who try their best. Yet this seems to happen in the handling of the parties in the Middle East conflict: Israel is clearly held to higher standards than its neighbors.

On the other hand, today's Israel is a high-tech country and, for this reason, economically very successful, which cannot be said of all Middle Eastern states. This may cause envy, but it should not be a reason to demand more from Israel than from others.

Many also seem to project their antipathies towards the Bible and Christianity onto Israel, which leads them to set high moral standards for the country. Christians who see Israel only as God's chosen people may have a part in this. Too often, Israel and its policies have been defended by appealing to the Bible.

The Bible does make it clear that the Jews are God's chosen people. Those who believe this do not need to close their eyes to the fact that Jews are only human and have done much wrong. This is clearly evident in the stories of the Bible, which honestly recount the wrongdoings committed by the chosen people both collectively and individually.

I will not list the evil deeds committed by the Jews as recounted in the Bible. However, it is clear to a Christian that the status of the chosen people is not based on the greater virtue of the Jews compared to others, but on God's choice. Those who believe this must accept God's decisions and His reasons for them. No human has the position to judge God Himself.

Believing that God has chosen Israel as His own people does not mean that all of Israel's actions should be accepted. Other countries have the right to express critical views. Unfortunately, the boundaries of justice and impartiality are easily crossed when dealing with Israel's actions.

It is often seen that the number of deaths caused by the conflict on both sides is compared. Typically, the situation has been that many more Palestinians have died than Israelis. Every death is regrettable, but it is not meaningful to compare the numbers of victims and set a goal of having an equal number of deaths on both sides.

Israel has a moral right to defend its territories from attackers who have publicly declared their goal to destroy the Jewish state. In defending itself, the country naturally uses its military forces, and a responsible government could not decide to allow a certain number of its own population to die before taking countermeasures.

If terrorists use the civilian population as human shields by establishing weapons depots, for example, in hospitals and children's daycare centers, causing a large number of innocent deaths, this is unfortunate, but it does not change the fact that the state of Israel has the right to exist.

I do not consider Israel to be the main culprit for the large number of civilian casualties when, for example, terrorists funded by Iran start a war. It is true that Jesus of Nazareth taught to turn the other cheek to the wrongdoer, but that advice can best be applied in one's own life.

No ethical conviction forbids protecting one's own civilians. If a person is willing to die for his pacifism, I believe they have the right to do so, but I cannot condemn those who choose to defend their own population.

Terrorists cynically use defenseless civilians as pawns in the propaganda war they have started. Therefore, when the term genocide is used, the correct target for the accusation is not on Israel's side.

Fortunately, Finland has not been involved in wars for a long time, and I hope peace continues. Our neighbors or those living within our borders do not question the right of our state to exist. If this happens in the future, only then can we give Israel advice on how to defend their country, but I suspect that at that time, Finns will also better understand those who are willing to fight for their land against aggressive neighbors.

I believe that Christian conviction does not oblige one to defend all political decisions made by the state of Israel, but I have no reason to condemn the Jewish state for using the means it deems necessary to defend itself.

George Roger Waters of the famous band Pink Floyd recently said that Jews living in Israel should move out of their country to achieve peace. Fortunately, this anti-Semitic stance is a rare reaction to the Middle East crisis in Western countries. Waters would hardly say the same if the existence of his own country were threatened.

I am concerned about how the facts related to Israel are easily forgotten when, for some reason, resentment and perhaps envy are felt towards Israel's economic success, and the country's ancient history is questioned.

From a Christian perspective, Israel is an extremely interesting country. The roots of Christianity are deeply embedded in Judaism, and Israel's role is likely to remain central in the future.

I am not sure how the events of the so-called end times will unfold. Those who know more than I claim that the end times already began 2000 years ago, and the scattering of Israel among other nations has represented dramatic phases in that era, but even more dramatic events are predicted to occur in the Holy Land in the indefinite future.

If the prophecies of the Bible come true in the future, as they have in many historical phases, the most significant upcoming event is likely to be the return of Jesus to earth and his reign over the world for 1,000 years, specifically from Israel.

I know that such ideas are often met with a smile, and I have seen and heard many wild and unfounded interpretations of the Bible in Pentecostalism, so I do not write this with great certainty. Still, it can be considered a great miracle that the state of Israel was re-established in 1948. This happened as a result of a political process, so one does not need to see anything supernatural in it unless he wants to, but it was a very rare event.

I cannot help but marvel at how things have progressed. I believe that the next phases of the story will also follow plans decided elsewhere than at human negotiation tables.

Angels

I have never seen angels, but it is easy for me to believe that they exist. When one finds it credible that a supernatural person first created the world, and then after witnessing how it all turned out came here to set things right by dying and rising again, a few angels are easy to accept intellectually.

The Bible contains many stories about angels, and they are depicted as not being particularly skilled at making jokes but rather seem completely focused on the tasks given to them. They cannot be blamed for this, as when God has given someone a task, it is probably worth completing before engaging in any other activities.

God also gave humans the task of cultivating and caring for the earth and multiplying and filling the earth. The latter task has been reasonably well taken care of, as there are already over 8 billion people. With the first task, however, we have faced serious challenges.

The first Christians were also given the task of spreading the gospel to the whole world. I assume that this task is still ongoing, especially as humanity continues to grow.

We Christians could learn from the angels, who know how to focus on what is essential. Angels are sometimes depicted with wings, which may symbolize their ability to move quickly from one place to another. However, this does not mean that we should strive to dart from continent to continent and from one mass event to another in our private jets, like some American megachurch preachers.

I do not know how well angels can empathize with humans. When they say their first sentence, it often seems to be "Do not be afraid!" This can mean understanding humans or a complete lack of situational awareness.

When a three-meter-tall glowing figure with a sword in hand suddenly stands in front of me, I naturally dare not be afraid if it is specifically forbidden. It is just as easy to smile freely at the owner of a Rottweiler who first praised his pet's 600-kilogram bite force and then urged not to be afraid because the dog would smell fear immediately.

But why does God need angels, as He is present everywhere in the universe at this very moment? Perhaps angels are just His calling cards, as humans probably could not withstand a direct encounter with Him.

God can certainly appear so subtly that humans do not even notice to be afraid. On the other hand, the Creator may sometimes want to show humans that the situation is serious by sending a heavenly army's highest-ranking general to say, "Do not be afraid!"

Perhaps the situation is a sign of God's sense of humor, even if the angel does not see anything amusing in it and the humans wet their pants. The Almighty God certainly has the right to act as He wishes. If people sometimes need to be scared for their own good, so be it.

Some people focus only on angels or rather on their own chosen perception of them: "Well, the God stuff is a bit too intense and demanding for my taste. And sins... I don't know. Somehow the Jesus story seems too bloody to be beautiful. And beauty is important to me. Glitter, the feather-light touch of the beyond now and then, the sweetness of grace, and the fleeting experience of life's meaning. And power without direction, just at my disposal, when tears of longing glisten on my cheeks. No difficult questions or even harder answers, just the rustle of protective wings around me."

In my opinion, this type of angel belief is not necessarily related to Christianity but is part of a broader new religiosity about which I am not qualified to say more.

However, in Christian circles, I have occasionally encountered such uncritical angel belief that deserves to be questioned. What can be said, for example, about a case where a person claimed to have seen an angel by the roadside at a time when he was proven to be indoors making Facebook updates? To top it off, he claimed there were other witnesses to the event, none of whom stepped forward to confirm the story.

I hope I am very wrong about this, but sometimes it seems as if some people see it as their mission to tell lies for the glory of God. When the Almighty clearly does not understand the hunger for the supernatural that plagues modern people languishing in dry rationality, can it be a grave sin to invent beautiful stories to strengthen people's faith?

Faith, hope, and love are all important, and the greatest of these is love. When writing about these virtues, Paul did not consider truth to be a less central value. As an Excel Christian, I want to believe everything that is true. Someone might say that faith is not needed if something is known to be true. This is correct, but it can also be said that the apostle of truth does not travel in the chariots of lies pulled by stolen horses.

The Bible

The books of the Bible were written over a long period of time. Perhaps none of the author thought that hundreds or thousands of years later, the texts would be compiled together and divided into separate chapters and verses. No one likely anticipated that the collection would be translated into thousands of languages and that many different translations would be produced for many of those languages.

The authors wrote what they considered essential in their texts without giving any thought to the fact that they would later be used for purposes often quite different from those for which they were originally written. The authors would have been astonished if someone from the present had traveled back in time and made it known that many texts should be written more precisely and logically, avoiding the names of animals and plants that would not be familiar thousands of years later, especially to those living in very different climates.

The authors were accustomed to the conflicts of their time and knew that not everyone would ever believe their works, but it would have been unpleasant for them to know that individual words and phrases would give rise to wars and divide people into groups that could not get along due to interpretive disagreements.

The authors would have been shocked to know that people in the future would argue about the different nuances of individual words that appeared only in some languages and translations and not at all in the original texts.

The authors would not have believed their ears if someone had told them that their texts would end up in books that would be considered almost magical objects, where every syllable breathed the presence of Holy God, even though some sentences had completely changed their meaning due to translation errors.

The original authors likely never considered the possibility that some in the future would make the holy book an infallible authority and the fourth person of the deity. They could not have understood the modern human's need to squeeze a bundle of ancient stories between leather covers adorned with gold letters.

Ancient people would not have guessed that their writings would one day be the last straw of absolute truth for many, preventing them from sinking into the swamp of postmodern relativism that surrounds them. They did not know that their texts would become the last and only reason for some to live.

The authors of the Bible could not have understood the roles their texts would later take on. They simply wrote what they believed to be true. They feared God and the king more than modern people, who are accustomed to questioning everything and laughing at political leaders who are ready to accept the light-hearted atmosphere of television talk shows and playful quizzes to be re-elected to their positions.

The authors of the Bible did not know they were producing texts for a holy book, but they believed their writings to be true before God and humans. They could not have even tried to foresee the possible objections of modern people or modify their texts to fit the constantly changing thought patterns of all future eras. They wrote about the events of their time, striving to stay true to the truth as they understood it.

The authors' honesty led them to describe many things that were problematic even in their own eyes, not to mention the readers. They wrote about facts as they were and did not, in modern style, first create a communication strategy, conduct a target group analysis, and then produce communication that was imagined to have the greatest possible impact.

The ancient authors of the Bible were, however, the best experts on their own texts and knew why they wrote them. They were above all honest, and that was and is the power of the texts. Modern people should not demand anything else from ancient people. We need the study of the Bible's texts and history to better understand their original purpose and meaning. If we do not understand them, the fault lies with us modern readers, not with the original texts or their authors.

The same uncompromising honesty is said to have been characteristic of the copyists of the Bible's texts, who were numerous before the invention of printing. I have no way to verify this myself, but literature has reported comparisons of texts copied at different times, which have shown the differences to be small.

It is much easier for me to believe in texts that have emerged through a human process, with numerous copies from different times found in various places and still available for viewing and study. For example, the Book of Mormon has a completely different origin story: It is said that one man found the golden plates on which the book was engraved. No one knows how the plates ended up in their hiding place, and the plates have not been found since.

One essential question is how the writings of the Bible ended up in the same collection. In Judaism, the writings that emerged before Christ have their own collections for Jews and Christians, with differences in the order and number of books. Christians call the collection the Old Testament, while Jews use the name Tanakh.

Texts that emerged after Christ were first compiled into the so-called New Testament in the second century, and the current list of books accepted into the Bible dates from the fourth century.

The Catholic Church has accepted more texts into its Bible than Protestants, both in the New and Old Testament. Therefore, there is no universally recognized Bible among all Christians. The fact that there has been no agreement on such a central issue underscores the human process that led to the creation of the book called the Bible.

For the reasons mentioned above, I believe there are no strong grounds to interpret the Bible literally. This does not mean, however, that the book is not true.

I will take the creation story as an example, where it is said that God created everything in a week. On the other hand, the same book says that for God, one day is like a thousand years and a thousand years like one day.

A literal interpretation of the creation of the universe could be that everything was created in one human calendar week, and the previous reference to God's different time scale might mean something else, such as that after the six thousand years of Earth's history, the seventh day begins, when God rests, i.e., the final period often called the millennium. Thus, two literal interpretations could be combined.

A non-literal interpretation could be that God created everything in one way or another, and we do not even know the length of God's time scale. When he commanded the earth to teem with living creatures, it happened. The essential thing is not how long the process took or what means he used. The essential thing is that he is behind everything. This is in no way contradictory to the scientific worldview, and no one can say in the name of science that the God outside the visible world could not have created everything visible.

When reading the Bible, one should not get caught up in trivial details, such as the fact that Paul seemed to accept slavery and urged Christian slaves to serve their masters conscientiously and not less diligently if the master was another believer.

Was it then right for Paul to approve of keeping slaves? It is perhaps difficult to know for sure. What is certain is that slavery or any other phenomenon or practice of society was not central to the core message of Christianity. The essential message was the forgiveness of sins through faith in Jesus Christ. Paul did not want to jeopardize the spread of this message by focusing on social reforms.

However, it can be understood that Paul at least considered the freeing of slaves to be good after a person who owned slaves began to follow Jesus. This is evident from Paul's letter to Philemon. And history shows that Christianity has played a central role in the abolition of slavery in the Western world, although in North America, slavery has sometimes also been justified with the Bible.

It may be difficult for modern people to even comprehend the nature of slavery, and it does not belong to our time and should not be accepted in any form. Still, it must be noted that few modern people are completely free to do as they wish.

Most people have to work to live, and there are various organizations, companies, supervisors, and leaders above them that they must serve. They are, however, usually free to change jobs on their own initiative, which was not possible for a slave.

In the same way, the Bible can be criticized for not defending the position of women sufficiently from a modern perspective. The same applies here as in the issue of slavery: The position of women was not and still is not the core issue of Christianity. It was not reasonable to jeopardize the success of the core message by mixing it with political issues.

What benefit would it have been for people if Christianity had only led to the resolution of all societal and temporary problems? All people would have eventually died without ever hearing the core message of Christianity, even if the structures of society had been reformed to perfection.

It was much wiser to let people first receive the message of salvation without demanding radical changes to societal structures, as once they received the message, they began to see social reforms as a development in line with Christianity.

The core message of the Bible is a timeless and culture-independent great story about how God seeks to get people to voluntarily come into contact with Him in the conditions they happen to be in. Everything else is secondary.

Are all religions equal?

It is often said that all religions lead to the same goal, whatever that may be. If a happy life on this planet is seen as the most important goal, then most religions can be said to at least strive to promote it. However, success in this can be weak either due to the misplaced demands within the religion itself or cultural constraints.

For example, if a religion includes a direct exhortation to convert people by force if necessary, this does not lead to increased happiness on earth. If the teachings of the religion are easily interpreted as a direct command to persecute those who believe differently, and the culture also supports such actions by, for example, inciting hatred between different population groups, it cannot be said that such a religion promotes the earthly well-being of all parties.

If a religion also denies the equal value of all people, social injustices are to be expected. On the other hand, if faith is so totally focused on the afterlife or the catastrophes threatening in this life that promoting material good and equality for all people is seen as futile or even harmful, it guides people towards a passivity that paralyzes societal development.

At best, however, all religions offer a general framework for understanding existence, some comfort in life's adversities, and the company of like-minded individuals. Understood in this way, many religions can be a positive force at both the individual and societal levels.

But is earthly good the only goal of religions? I think this is rarely the case. I certainly cannot claim to know all the major world religions well, but it seems to me that the reality awaiting a person after death is depicted very differently in different religions and even in different branches of the same religion.

If the set goal is not the same at all, it is at best careless and at worst offensive to claim that all religions lead to the same outcome. The goals set by some religions are then said to remain unattainable or are labeled as wrong. I suspect that the images of the afterlife in different religions only appear similar to those who reject all promises of life after death.

I emphasize that I do not even try to make sense of the descriptions of the afterlife in perhaps thousands of religions worldwide, but I briefly address a couple of examples. For instance, the difference between Christianity and Buddhism is vast. A Christian believes or hopes to go to heaven to be with a loving God, while the ideal in Buddhism is enlightenment or nirvana, where a person's suffering ends through the extinguishing of the thirst for life, without any gods involved.

The Muslim paradise seems to be designed more for men than for women and appears to promise a more perfect version of earthly happiness rather than a spiritual dimension. Islam also teaches that entry into paradise is based on strict adherence to religious laws, but Allah still reserves the right to make arbitrary decisions about whether a person is admitted to paradise or condemned to hell.

The conceptions of God are thus quite different, as are the views on sins and good deeds. Buddhism does not teach anything about gods and is sometimes considered to be a philosophical approach rather than a religion. This is emphasized by the fact that some adherents of Buddhism may declare themselves atheists.

Judaism, Christianity, and Islam teach that only one God exists. In Christianity, however, the idea of God's three persons (Father, Son, and Holy Spirit) is very central. Jews and Muslims absolutely reject the divinity of Jesus, while in Christianity, there is the central claim that Christ was both human and God.

The differences between religions could be listed endlessly, but my competence and the scope of this book do not allow for a deep comparison. What I consider essential is that it is an insult to most religions to claim that they are fundamentally the same. Their views are rather in such irreconcilable conflict with each other that they cannot all logically be true.

Logically, it is possible that no religion represents the truth, but it may also be that only one of them is correct. However, not all their claims can be true at the same time.

I am a Christian and believe that Christianity teaches the core message correctly. This does not mean that everything historically or currently associated with Christianity is part of it. If the autumn wind carries yellow birch leaves through the open window or door of a church, they will never become part of Christianity, even if they are never cleaned up but allowed to accumulate under the carpets spread in the church aisles, in the priests' robes, and between the pages of Bibles.

Christianity is also unique in many ways, just like all other religions. The peculiarity of Christianity is that it claims God loves the humans He created so much that He sacrificed Himself to atone for their evil deeds. Such claims are rarely heard.

Even politicians who love hyperbole and seek power rarely, if ever, go so far in their words and actions as to voluntarily allow themselves to be killed. The cruel execution of a dissident who has languished as a political prisoner, been on a hunger strike, or been tortured is not comparable to the death of Jesus. In Jesus' case, it was about the voluntary suffering of God Himself.

Yes, the death of many people can be said to have been noble and self-sacrificing, but Jesus rose from the dead, which no other representative of a religious or political movement has done. It was the resurrection that proved Jesus to be God. This is what I want to believe, and I think there are good reasons for this belief, even though it is impossible to present conclusive proof during this life.

However, religions can also be approached from a game-theoretical perspective, although I do not suggest incorporating the model I am about to present into sacred traditions. The first premise is that all religions accept good deeds done for the benefit of others, and according to some, these are even the most important for a person's fate in the afterlife. A follower of Jesus should live rightly and do good, so with good luck, a Christian will pass the tests of all other religions and reach as good a place after death as each religion dares to promise.

Christianity is an exception in this regard: Good deeds do not guarantee a place in heaven; people must believe in Jesus if they wish to go there. The only way to enter the Christian heaven is to be a Christian. Representatives of no other religion are accepted into heaven based solely on their good deeds, but a Christian might easily enter the heavens of other religions based on their quota of good deeds.

From a game-theoretical perspective, it is therefore worth being a Christian if one wants to maximize his chances of eternal happiness. Success in the pursuit of earthly happiness has been considerably weaker for Christians at many times and in various cultures. But a person's earthly life lasts only a few tens of thousands of days, while eternity in heaven lasts, well, an eternity. A person should indeed be ready to give up what he cannot keep anyway to gain something better that he can never lose.

Finally, a few words on the often-asked question of how on earth those living outside the reach of Christianity could believe in Jesus and be saved. Most of the world's people are born outside of Christian culture, and despite missionary work, not everyone may ever hear anything about Christianity.

I must admit that I do not know the answer to this difficult question. Still, I am inclined to believe in God's justice. He sees and knows everyone's thoughts. We humans do not.

For some reason, we have been given us the message. I believe we thus have a greater duty to bring the message to those who are unaware of it than they have to come to us seeking it. At the very least, we cannot claim that we have not been told about Jesus if we decide to reject him against better knowledge.

In matters other than faith, we would hardly ignore valuable guidance offered to us, even if we did not know how others would fare. Therefore, it is unlikely that anyone would act in the following manner related to a more mundane situation:

"A man went berry picking in the forest and encountered many other walkers along the way, but he was able to be alone most of the time according to his own preferences. He didn't even see others, and he whistled quietly.

Suddenly, he saw something white flicker on a blueberry patch in front of him. He bent down to examine what he saw and found it to be a small piece of paper. He stretched his tired back with a sigh and stood up, holding the paper between his fingers.

He read: 'Notice: On July20th, this forest will be burned by the decision of the Ministry of the Environment to prevent the spread of pests. People are advised to stay out of the forest on that day.'

The man glanced at his phone and was startled, as the date was exactly 20.7. For some reason, the man first poured the berries from the bucket onto the ground, not knowing what else to do. Then he began to walk feverishly back and forth, thinking about what to do.

He wondered if other berry pickers had also found the notice somewhere in the berry bushes. He remembered how randomly he himself had noticed the piece of paper. He stopped to think but did not recall ever seeing a similar announcement in the newspaper. He only used to read the sports pages, though.

Could a leaflet explaining the matter have fallen through the home's mail slot? He didn't remember seeing such a thing. At the same time, he realized that years ago, he had put a sign next to the mail slot that unequivocally prohibited all free distribution.

Good heavens! The man decided to immediately go warn other berry pickers just in case. He took a few brisk steps but suddenly stopped, realizing he didn't know in which direction the nearest other person had been or if he was still there. And he had seen many people in the forest that day. The man was startled to realize that he could never warn everyone, even if he started shouting wildly around him.

The man concluded that it was most sensible to walk towards his car while shouting as loud as his lungs could bear. Then he suddenly became furious: 'It's outrageous how poorly such a big and important matter has been communicated!' There should have been large signs at the edge of the forest telling about the danger, but he didn't remember seeing any.

The man lamented how unjust everything was: Maybe he was the only one in this forest who knew what was happening. Why should he be the one to start warning others? He had never been the type to shout even at football matches. He had always felt embarrassed watching otherwise orderly and reserved men childishly riot in the stands.

And was such forest burning even legal? He dug his phone out of his pocket and tried to call the only lawyer he knew, who happened to be his nephew. Well, of course, there wasn't enough signal for the phone in the forest. The man slipped it into his pocket and looked at the notice again. Only now did he notice it: There was no space after the 'July' and '20th'. There was an error in the text! He examined and turned the paper again. Suddenly he was sure of what he should have realized immediately: Someone was playing a prank on him.

No one could really just burn the forest, neglect communication so poorly, and even leave out an essential space in the text! How on earth had he fallen for such a trick?

The man continued picking berries but was in an irritated mood. Even the birds around seemed to mock him. Grumbling, he put on his headphones and started listening to music on his phone.

The bucket was only half full when he noticed that the trees were on fire all around him. He first looked around in panic, then started running quickly but stumbled over a root and fell on his stomach.

The man felt the heat as his synthetic jacket caught fire, but the smoke soon mercifully filled his lungs, interrupted the oxygen supply to his brain, and he sensed nothing more."

Climate change

Climate change seems like a credible threat, and I am not qualified to question its reality. However, I find it difficult to trust that the climate models used to make predictions are as accurate as the masses are led to believe.

Scientists themselves are aware of the great uncertainties associated with all modeling, but discussions about uncertainties become secondary when things are simplified to advance political goals.

I do believe that the main political goal is to combat climate change, but there are a whole host of other intertwined objectives. States, companies, and political parties are trying to use the ongoing climate crisis to advance their own interests.

States are negotiating climate agreements that they believe will bring them relative advantage. Companies, on the other hand, are striving to succeed in building new industries and other climate-related businesses. And political parties are trying to profile themselves as well as possible in the eyes of their voters to at least maintain their power, if not improve their positions.

In science, it has not been customary to vote on the truth, but in the international climate panel (IPCC), this is reportedly happening. This underscores the fact that the climate issue is highly politicized.

Since it is understandably desired to get large masses of people to accept the necessity of lifestyle changes, complex and uncertain scientific findings and theories have been replaced with crude simplifications. In the name of political expediency, the truth has been compromised. It is not communicated clearly how uncertain the calculations are.

Combating climate change has become an ideology: Scientists or media representatives quoting them make predictions about the future that they cannot prove to be correct. And none of them need to be around in 2100 to comment on the accuracy or lack thereof of the calculation models' results. Yet, those who question the claims are labeled as backward opponents of progress.

The greatest uncertainty, in my opinion, relates to people's ability to stop the rise in the Earth's temperature. Most of the attempts to reduce the use of fossil fuels have been made in wealthy regions, which, however, produce only a portion of the planet's total carbon dioxide emissions.

Developing economies do not necessarily have to follow all the bad examples of rich countries; they can move more directly to lifestyles that are better balanced with the environment. Still, it is unrealistic to expect them to voluntarily remain poor to save our shared planet.

During the COVID pandemic, we learned to replace many business trips with telecommunication-based meetings, but the volume of air traffic has already exceeded the pre-pandemic level. This may be an important reason for the likely failure to stop the climate change.

As long as the fuels needed for airplanes are produced from oil, fossil fuels suitable for cars will inevitably also be produced. No profit-seeking company will voluntarily store them as unusable hazardous waste but will try to sell them at some price.

At the same time, as traffic in rich countries becomes electrified, more fossil fuels will begin to be used elsewhere. And the carbon dioxide produced in developing countries ends up in the same shared atmosphere, just as granting the right to urinate in one corner of a swimming pool would lead to the contamination of the entire pool.

There has been talk of synthetic fuels for airplanes, but nothing concrete has happened yet, and the goals are modest. The aim is only that in the future, even a small part of airplane fuels could be synthetic.

On the other hand, the batteries needed for electric cars require a significant increase in the production of certain metals and the opening of new mines, resulting in environmental destruction.

People have many reasons to be skeptical about the talk of beating the climate change. One such reason is that not all those who keep it in the spotlight seem to believe in reducing carbon dioxide emissions themselves, as most conferences in the field are still held as physical events, even though some climate researchers have significantly reduced their flying.

In climate discussions, it is often left unsaid how much carbon dioxide emissions have decreased. The reason for this silence is obvious: Emissions were higher in 2024 than ever before, and the trend has consistently been upward. Only in individual years of economic recession have emissions sometimes decreased compared to the previous year, but soon they have risen again to higher levels than before.

My own view is that the climate change will not be successfully stopped. At best, it can only be slowed down enough to allow adaptation to it.

Some scientists and politicians see climate change as threatening the existence of humanity. Therefore, they do not hesitate to paint bleak future scenarios, presumably to draw attention to their ideas and influence political decisions of states.

I do not oppose combating climate change as part of environmental protection, but I sincerely hope that climate change never becomes such a central issue that other environmental challenges are excessively sidelined.

What could be a more apocalyptic future scenario than one rising from the Book of Revelation? But if Revelation holds true, humanity will not be destroyed as a result of climate change. However, every individual will inevitably die someday, and that is humanity's greatest existential question. Compared to that, climate change is a small detail. No one should let it interfere with solving that greater question for themselves.

End times

Everything that begins at some point will end later. The truth of this statement can be confirmed by everyone's own experiences. A good thing, like a vacation, ends all too quickly. A tedious speech at a celebration, on the other hand, seems to go on and on, but it too eventually ends.

A person also understands that they will die someday. And they know that everything else follows the same pattern: a beginning, a middle phase, and an end. Biological life on this planet, good and bad political systems, even the entire universe will end someday because they all began at some point.

Naturally, it is not easy to define or know the exact moment of origin for all temporal phenomena, but such a moment exists. At some point, the first living cell must have been created, at some moment a decision-maker must have lifted their pen from the paper after signing the founding document of a new state or political party. And at some moment, a fetus must have completely emerged from its mother's body and become a baby legally, so that the midwife could write the child's birth time in a notebook with a ballpoint pen, accurate to the minute.

The time of a person's death can be quite easily understood as the moment when the heart beats for the last time. But it is not always easy to define the end of all things as precisely. For example, the dissolution of the Roman Empire took hundreds of years, and one day it was simply noted that it no longer existed, but entirely different rulers had taken its place.

When the New Testament of the Bible speaks of the last days, it becomes clear to the reader that the authors who lived 2000 years ago believed the end of everything was very near and most likely would happen during their lifetime. And they cannot be blamed for this, as they, like all other people before and after them, have lived in very special times. The entire world known to the first Christians was ruled by Rome, known for its brutal tactics, and at some point, the emperors began to be declared gods upon their burial.

Naturally, Christians did not conform to the Roman imperial cult, and they began to be persecuted. In the eyes of Christians, the time was very evil. It was quite natural to assume that the end of everything was near, especially since Jesus himself had urged them to be ready for his imminent return.

This tradition has continued for 2000 years. At all times, there have been enough signs of human wickedness and other threats to make the idea of Jesus' imminent return and the ensuing end of the world comforting to Christians. Wars have raged almost constantly somewhere, and the worst pandemic in history was likely the Black Death in the 14th century, which resulted in the death of a third or even half of Europeans.

The pace has only accelerated in the so-called modern era. In the 20th century, two world wars were fought, and in the 1940s, people learned to make atomic bombs, and for the first time in history, humanity had the possibility of total destruction at the push of a button.

In 1948, the state of Israel was re-established, which has been an important sign of the times for many Christians. Various phases of other nations have also often been seen as omens of the approaching end of everything.

Alongside the threat of total nuclear war, the limited natural resources of the planet in relation to the ever-growing population have become a factor threatening the existence of all humanity. The third and most recent addition to the existential threats facing humanity is climate change, which is said to be largely caused by the warming of the planet due to the increase in atmospheric carbon dioxide levels.

Of the causes of total destruction, nuclear war is the least speculative: We know for sure that humanity is capable of destroying itself with atomic weapons. There have been no differing views on this. The depletion of natural resources and continuous population growth are not as straightforward and certain threats, as the need for raw materials changes with technology, and their availability is impossible to predict accurately because new deposits are still being discovered.

Climate change is a fact in the light of statistics, and the only uncertainty is humanity's ability to stop it. The possibilities look bleak.

So, people today, as before, have great problems to solve. What is new is that the most pessimistic prophecies are now being made by secular scientists, while Christians still see hope. When researchers warn of the possibility of total destruction, a believer in the Bible can justifiably give others this advice: "Don't panic but make sure you find Jesus. Your soul is in a greater danger than this planet".

The most significant part of the Bible dealing with the end times, the Book of Revelation, does not predict total destruction for this planet or its life. The environmental disasters predicted in Revelation are indeed catastrophic in their scope, but the main concern is human wickedness: Even in the face of great suffering, humanity is not willing to turn to their Creator and ask for forgiveness for their evil deeds. Those who are willing to repent, however, will be persecuted by the Antichrist, who holds power over the entire world, and they will be killed. Nevertheless, their souls will be saved.

All these horrors occur during the so-called time of wrath, which lasts only seven years. Christians interpret Revelation in many different ways. Some believe that Jesus will first secretly take the believers away from the world. This is called the rapture. Only after this, many Christians believe, will the time of wrath begin. Others believe that even the believers will have to go through the entire time of wrath or at least part of it.

Some, however, believe that Revelation contains no predictions relevant for our modern times, but that everything described refers to the ancient Roman Empire or is a symbolic depiction of the spiritual struggles of believers.

I do not consider myself qualified to take a stance on these interpretative disagreements, but I still take the Book of Revelation seriously. When looking at world events, it is easy to believe that the end of everything is near. However, the Book of Revelation clearly contains a lot of symbolism, and I do not know which parts are meant to be taken literally, if any.

Many things have improved in recent decades, at least in Western countries. For example, healthcare and investment in environmental protection are in better shape than before. Individual freedoms have increased.

However, human life today is increasingly artificial, virtual, and detached from biological reality. Most professions are far from natural if understood as the direct fulfillment of biological needs.

Food can be ordered online, and only a few are still capable of farming or slaughtering livestock themselves. I, too, am an inept city dweller who would be among the first to perish if our complex societal structure suddenly collapsed and food distribution chains ceased to function.

Scientists have studied the rise and fall of ancient cultures, and they all seem to have become increasingly complex as their end approached. Our own time fits this characteristic well. This does not necessarily mean that the entire history of the world is heading towards a quick end. It is possible that several civilizations will follow after us. However, I consider this unlikely for two reasons.

Firstly, despite significant regional cultural differences, our world is in many ways an interconnected whole that is more dependent on technology than any previous civilization. Humanity has never before held so many self-produced poison pills of total destruction in its hand, nor has it ever come as close to the purely physical limits of growth set by the planet.

And as I wrote at the very beginning, everything ends sometime. Some civilization must eventually be the last. But I believe that none of us will ever cease to exist. Each individual must choose during their lifetime how he relates to their Creator, on whom they are fundamentally and completely dependent, whether they want to be or not.

Heaven

It is difficult to define what heaven is, and it may not even be possible. Everyone probably has their own image of heaven. Over time, different words have been invented in various languages to describe God and His dwelling place, heaven, but it seems that these two concepts have been very closely connected. Wikipedia claims that the Finnish word "taivas" (heaven) is based on the Latin word "Deus," meaning God.

In Finnish, the physical sky, where clouds float and birds soar, is the same word as God's abode, which is not the case in some other languages I know. The use of the same word is natural, as the physical sky is seen from a human perspective as being above, and it has been natural for humans to think that the highest authority in the universe is also somewhere above them.

Of course, it is difficult to draw an equal sign between spiritual and physical height, remembering that the Earth floats in space, where no direction is more up or down than any other. In space, one can just as well speak of depth as of height. In more spiritual language, depth, height, and space are sometimes almost the same thing: Wisdom or thought can be great when it is deep, high, or vast. In contrast, lowliness, baseness, smallness, and narrowness are often seen as opposites.

It is easy to see that heaven and God are concepts so intertwined that they sometimes become synonymous in language. When one says "Heaven, protect us!", they are asking for protection from God. Heaven would not be heaven if it were empty and God were not there.

Similarly, the location of leaders and the power they represent are often equated. For example, when the news reports that the Kremlin has taken a certain stance, it naturally refers to the Russian leadership operating there, not primarily to the large fortress.

Secular concepts have emerged alongside the spiritual heaven in everyday language, originating from higher meanings. Food in a fine restaurant can be described as heavenly good, or a large and well-equipped shopping center might be called a shopping paradise. Yet, the real heaven is one where a higher God than money resides, and even the best chef's creations are not truly heavenly.

Heavenly dimensions do not fit into earthly words, and heavenly nature refuses to be flattened into earthly terms. Heaven is not part of any visible reality, nor can it be scientifically studied. Heaven is not a club where one can get a VIP card by knowing the right people. One can only hope to enter by knowing the right God.

What is heaven like then? Is everything there boring, oppressively tedious, and holy? Is it only permissible to lie prostrate before the greatness that constantly wants to be reminded of its eternal wisdom, mercy, and infinite love? Is eternity in heaven like Good Friday at grandma's house, when it's sleeting outside and you have to be quiet inside while grandma tries to recover from her migraine attack?

Or does the heavenly air vibrate with goodness that I never knew existed? Am I surrounded there by love that removes all fear, lifts me gently onto its palm without crushing me, like a good person lifts a sparrow with a broken wing, and tells me that I am finally at home and safe?

Does the brightness of wisdom shine everywhere I look? A brightness that does not dazzle but allows me to see everything for the first time in all its beauty?

Is heaven eternal goodness, where I wake up from decades of nightmares? A refuge whose door is opened to me, the homeless, after crawling my whole life with bloody knees on pitch-dark alleys echoing with the laughter of devils, fearing the approaching scrape of beasts' claws, listening anxiously to the whimpering of their sniffing snouts, and fearing the greedy breath of their steaming jaws?

Is heaven brightness without shadows, a smile without bitterness and cynicism, the light's answer to the darkness's questions, an answer that silences the demonic accusations of my enemies and the last temptations of my own heart? Can I leave my worn-out overalls, reeking of gasoline, vomit, and feces, in the trash bin outside the heavenly spa and, after washing, wrap myself in a white bathrobe?

If I ever get to partake in all that without any merits of my own, I believe that then I will fully understand that human salvation is entirely God's accomplishment.

And I believe it to be true: Compared to God, a human is insignificant, for he would not even exist if he had not been created by someone greater. And they are not fundamentally good, but despite this, God Himself has, for some reason, wanted to go through all the trouble to save as many of their kind as possible.

Heaven would not be heaven without God, and perhaps it would not have been built at all if humans had not been destined from the beginning to live there with God. A human is therefore helpless and small compared to God, but not useless. The entire cosmic-level mega-spectacle was initiated for the sake of humans, but of course, by God's will.

God might theoretically have chosen otherwise and said to Himself: "Listen, I don't think I'll bother to start designing those humans after all. I am simply not that kind of God. Oh, right, there are no other gods, but I understand my own point: Humans would probably only bring sorrow and trouble."

God could have created different cosmoses for His timeless amusement and played with big bangs until He got bored, and how can we know that He didn't do just that. It might have been quite enjoyable to develop domino tracks the size of universes and multiverses and watch how the process progresses with different sets of initial setups.

But when one has done all this throughout his entire eternal life, surely anyone would hope for someone else to say something like this at some point: "What an explosion! I would call that a show, for it had so much color, brilliance, and drama."

God might have thought something like that until an eternal smile spread from the beginning of timelessness to its infinitely distant end and from one immaterial boundlessness to the next. God may have first created a shirt so He could roll up His sleeves and then proclaimed to Himself: "Let us make man and build heaven suitable for him."

God is called Father. Anyone who has own children knows how much he or she loves them and is willing to do everything for their happiness. Anyone who has had or still has good parents, or at least one, knows what it is like to be the child of a good parent.

If one believes that humans are created in the image of God, it is easy to see that the affection between a good parent and their child originates from the eternal God and from a time before time.

When one acknowledges the smallness of a human being compared to the Creator of the universe, he is convinced that the love and goodness shown between earthly parents and their children are invaluable but only fleeting glimpses of something much greater, more perfect, and more beautiful. That great, ultimate, and eternal awaits us in heaven. I want to get there one day!

Hell

Flames and unbearable heat are often associated with the idea of hell. Even those who do not believe in the reality of such a place or state have this image of hell. The same description is found in the teachings of Jesus of Nazareth.

Even modern people who believe in the reality of hell often consider the descriptions to be strongly metaphorical. Firstly, a person's physical body would soon cease to exist in such conditions: It would simply burn away.

In a physical worldview, sensing heat requires the functioning of a person's nervous system. Thus, only the soul could remain in such conditions, but how on earth could the soul sense physical heat?

Thinking this way, the heat must be a metaphor for something else. The human body could not endure any conditions forever. Therefore, the concept of hell must be metaphorical in the mind of modern people.

I am not sure what to think myself, as the doctrine of hell originated before the modern scientific worldview. For a person who believes that God created everything out of nothing, it is easy to think that the same Creator could also easily give a person a body that endures any conditions without the mercy of physical death.

On the other hand, I believe in the eternity of the soul, so I can just as well think that the sufferings of hell are directed precisely at the soul. But for someone who believes that physical reality came about by chance without the influence of any supernatural factor, it is probably impossible to take seriously even the existence of an eternal soul, let alone its eternal suffering.

The most essential question for most seems to be this: How could a loving God condemn a person to eternal suffering? This is the reason many choose not to believe in God at all, which can be seen as a fallacy: The most essential question is whether God exists or not. Whether I like Him or not is entirely secondary to that first question.

God does not cease to exist if I do not like Him, but it may be possible for me to declare my life a God-free zone. If I reject God, I have the right to do so. If I decide that I never want to have anything to do with God, He will not forcibly enter my life but will allow my immortal soul to be separated from Him for eternity.

So, God does not necessarily condemn me to eternal hell, but I have the power to demand a final separation from Him. However, I was not created in such a way that I can manage without God. If I try to live this earthly life on my own, it is possible, but it will cause me suffering.

During this physical life, I do not have to be completely alone, as I get to enjoy the entire world created by God and especially the company of other people. And since people are created in the image of God, I am never entirely separated from God's influence as long as I live. But when I die, I lose contact with the world created by God and with other people. Then I will face a final separation from God if that is what I have wanted. And this causes immense suffering in a person who is meant to be in communion with God.

It is often claimed that hell is actually equivalent to eternal separation from God. C.S. Lewis has said that a person is given a lifetime to learn to humbly say to God, "Your will be done." If a person never agrees to this and wants to be the god and ruler of his own life, eventually God has to say to the person, "Your will be done."

So, it can be said that a person condemns himself to hell if the idea that hell is separation from God holds true. However, one can ponder whether it is possible that a person, once in hell, might change his mind. Perhaps he realizes that he would rather be with God than separated from Him. How would God respond to such a situation? Would it be too late to repent?

I have no theory about whether one can still repent in hell. Naturally, I have to leave the decision to God, even though He does not need my consent for anything. Still, I feel compelled to ask, how can one know if anyone would want to leave hell once he is there?

It is clear that the conditions in hell are unbearable, but does anyone who ends up there ever admit he made the wrong choice? Could anyone in that situation still humble himself? And could God even transfer a person from hell to heaven? Perhaps it is logically impossible. Even the Almighty cannot do everything imaginable, such as making one plus one equal three or five.

I believe that there is an absolute and objective reality, even if I may never understand it. In that reality, things simply are a certain way: One plus one is two, and the leaves of trees rustle in the wind, even if no one is listening. Perhaps in that objective and absolute reality, the road to hell is wide and one-way, and no one ever comes back from there.

Maybe some things are simply final and permanent. Possibly, a person's eternal fate does not have a one or two-week return policy typical of online store products.

Who can be sure of such things? The incomprehensible size of the universe and its age, which seems eternal compared to human physical life, speak seriously in favor of the view that the universe does not revolve around humans and does not operate on their terms.

Although a person may wish for something as intensely as possible when seeing a shooting star, the wish will likely remain a dream unless some greater processes are already moving in the direction the person desires. Most people readily accept their minor role in the cosmic play. Why would hell and heaven be tailored to each person's wishes?

It is safest to assume that the rules written by God are not negotiable but remain valid as long as God wills. If one wants to avoid hell and reach heaven, it is advisable to take the instructions of the highest authority seriously and submit all required documents to the heavenly office by the deadline, rather than wasting time on doomed appeal processes.

Near death experiences

People have occasionally had unusual experiences when they have been near death or when their heart has even stopped completely before being revived. Some have seen a bright tunnel, some heaven or hell. However, some have not experienced anything or at least have not remembered sensing anything upon waking up.

Do such experiences have evidential value? I do not underestimate the fact that returning from the brink of death surely feels like a serious message in itself, even if it also means getting a new opportunity. The experience must be even more dramatic if one has sensed something fantastic or terrifying.

I also do not have the qualifications to question the authenticity of people's stories, even though some have later admitted to fabricating at least part of what they told. And who am I to claim that the Almighty could not, if desired, speak to a person through such an experience.

On the other hand, I know that people's brains are extraordinarily complex, and I have not heard or read of any researcher claiming that the physiology of the brain is already thoroughly known. I am not a brain researcher, but I have great respect for the ordinary human brain, even if it is examined only as matter and a complex biological mechanism.

I also know that some people have exceptional abilities due to natural talent and practice, which are almost impossible for others to understand. Examples of this include people blessed with enormous memory capacity or remarkable intelligence, as well as those who master a musical instrument with virtuoso precision and confidence.

Even the experiences of normal life for us ordinary people are astonishing if we take a moment to think about them. The vast capacity of the brain and its central role in everything a person does are undeniable. A positive example of this is the astonishingly rapid learning of a healthy child. A negative example is the varying degrees of loss of cognitive and motor abilities due to a brain disease.

In this context, it is necessary to mention the concept of consciousness, awareness, and self that lives in all of us. I have heard from those who know more than I do that the connection between such experiences and the biological functioning of the brain is not fully understood. And even if a researcher inclined towards materialism claims that all such experiences are merely illusions and that everything can be explained through biological, physical, and chemical processes, I trust my own, rather than another's, illusions.

It is indisputably clear to me that I think and am aware of it. If I cannot trust this, how could I trust a researcher who claims that people live in illusions but still believes they can think clearly enough to recognize illusions and hallucinations, at least in others.

It is easy for me to believe in the Bible's revelation on this matter as well. The fact that humans were created in the image of God probably means at least that humans experience a sense of self. God also declared His name to be "I am."

Humans, therefore, have consciousness, the nature of which scientists are free to debate, but I personally believe that consciousness resides in the brain during this earthly life. This does not mean that human consciousness is not dependent on something external.

It is impossible to prove this right or wrong, but what if we are conscious only because God allows it? If He wanted to take our consciousness away, He could probably do so as easily as a person picks a raspberry from a bush. He could take away our biological life at any time, so why not everything else as well?

But perhaps God has decided to let us be conscious beings forever, once we have become such. Against this background, it is easy to think that such consciousness, independent of brain function, could manifest when a person approaches the brink of death. However, I do not think the matter is that straightforward.

Although humans are said to be made in the image of God, we are very imperfect in that state, constantly making cognitive errors, and our heads are said to be full of false memories. I once heard a brain researcher suggest that today's event will already have generated the first false memory by tomorrow.

I cannot be entirely sure about this either, as my life is not constantly studied nor its events carefully documented. My brain is free to be filled with false memories if I do not share them with others and thus expose my perceptions to others' criticism. Still, I do not believe that everything I experience is an illusion.

My brain may understand reality mostly correctly, even if it occasionally falls into serious errors. If this is the case, it makes scientific research possible in my view. The danger of random thought errors is likely significantly smaller when many researchers ponder the same problem and discuss it. Of course, this does not protect against systematic errors, which could result from the general inability of all humans to see some things correctly.

It is known that most people can be deceived by sleight of hand tricks and optical illusions. Therefore, it would not be far-fetched to think that making some scientific observations reliably might be impossible for humans. No human may be able to detect such a general human weakness.

Then to the original question: Can observations made near the brink of death be trusted? I dare not say anything definitive about this, but I do not trust these accounts any more than dreams.

Even if consciousness independent of the human brain were a reality, brain function inevitably comes into play as soon as a person revives. At that point, the perceptions formed during a person's life, a few sensory observations, interpretations produced by the brain, and possibly some truly supernatural experience may all converge. There is simply no way to know the significance of each factor.

I have no experience of being near death. But one day, I will have the certain experience of crossing that boundary, just like everyone else. I want to be as ready as a person can be when that time comes.

Perhaps the most important message from near-death experiences is this: Be ready, for one day you will cross that boundary without ever returning.

Suffering

How can a loving God allow all suffering? Can I even believe in the existence of such a God when I know what is happening in the world every moment? This so-called problem of suffering is an important reason for many to reject claims of a good God.

Various arguments have been presented in favor of the possibility of the simultaneous existence of suffering and a loving God, and they have always seemed more convincing to me than attempts to reject belief in God by citing the prevalence and senselessness of suffering.

I admit that the existence of suffering feels bad to me too. It is especially difficult for me to accept the horrors that innocent children too often have to endure. I believe most people think the same way, and I believe it is the common duty of all people to strive to minimize all kinds of suffering.

Positive developments have occurred on many fronts, although it is not always easy to believe when following the news in the media. Medicine and healthcare have advanced tremendously, even though diseases cannot be completely eradicated.

Of course, things are not nearly as good everywhere in the world as they are in many of the modern countries. On the other hand, suffering does not seem to be close to ending in any country.

Some suffering is senseless and seems pointless, without anyone to blame for it. Examples of this include illnesses that affect people who take good care of their health. These seem to lack credible explanations, leading people to attribute them to an all-powerful God.

On the other hand, people deliberately or negligently cause pain to each other, and I don't think human evil deeds can be blamed on God. Still, it is often asked why God doesn't prevent the atrocities committed by humans. I believe the explanation lies in the fact that the Creator has given us free will, and many misuse this gift. The fault is not God's.

It can certainly be argued that giving free will to evil people represented a lack of judgment on God's part. However, the truth is that all people are evil if circumstances are bad or even if they are ideal. This is one of the messages of the Bible's story of the fall: People living in ideal conditions often do wrong. No human has the ability to make just demands of God and advise Him, because humans themselves are evil.

Since God has clearly given humans free will, humans have no choice but to strive to use their freedom in good ways. However, I believe in a just universe and that each of us will ultimately be held accountable for every action we take.

A person is also responsible for those living close to him and has a duty to protect the weak to the best of his ability. This is done through police and judicial systems as well as social services. The laws that guide all of this are enacted through democratic processes in many countries. If we believe that unsuitable people have been selected as members of parliament, we are collectively responsible for this.

God should not be blamed if people pass bad laws, especially if citizens dissatisfied with political processes are not ready to participate in political activities themselves.

However, bad things undeniably happen, and not everyone accepts the explanation of free will given to humans. The problem of suffering can, however, be seen as a strong argument for the existence of a good God.

It is entirely reasonable to ask what the expectation that justice should prevail and that the innocent should not suffer is based on. I am sure that evolution theorists can find speculative explanatory models for this ideal of justice.

One could argue that a society that protects the weak is stronger than a system based on oppression, and that the success of our species is partly due to this. This claim cannot be proven true. Equally, one could think that pity is weakness and that those who succeed in competition are justified and even obliged to use their power and strength to eliminate weaker individuals.

However, the idea that suffering and evil should not exist and that it is honorable to make sacrifices to fight them, both individually and societally, seems to be a common thought among all humans. I believe this attitude is a distant echo across all cultures from a time before the fall into sin. Humans are evil, but they still remember what goodness is.

Despite their wickedness, humans are still made in the image of a good God. A broken image that, even in its shattered state, fundamentally knows the position it was originally created and placed in. They know the ideal of goodness, but their evil nature is evident in that they demand higher morality from others than from themselves. And they prefer to blame their Creator rather than themselves.

Human corruption is also evident in that, although their high ideals remind them of their origin as God's image and they can recognize suffering as an alien and contrary phenomenon to the original plan, they use the very existence of suffering as an argument against belief in God.

We must do everything we can to minimize suffering in this world, even though we know it will never disappear from our lives during our earthly journey. The most important thing, however, is to understand that suffering can, at best, draw us into communion with God, even though we are all tempted to use it as evidence against God, even when we have caused our suffering ourselves.

Is my faith a private matter?

In different Christian denominations, there are varying traditions regarding how actively an individual is expected to share their faith with others. In denominations that emphasize a personal decision, the ideal is to spread the gospel as actively as possible, while in Christianity that emphasizes the grace of infant baptism and God's choice, this may not be seen as equally necessary.

I believe it is quite likely that Christianity would never have spread worldwide if the early church had kept their faith a private matter. From the beginning, the first Christians faced persecution, but Jesus did not leave them any freedom of choice when he gave them the direct command to take the message "to all the world," which at that time primarily meant the Roman Empire. The Bible mentions that Paul at least planned to travel to Spain, and legends claim that Thomas did missionary work in India. What is certain is that Christianity soon began to be spread around the planet, although too often as part of a political agenda and colonialism. At worst, those posing as Christians forced pagans to be baptized at gunpoint.

However, I am inclined to believe that not all missionary work has ever been done with a sword in hand. There have likely always been sincere proclaimers of the message of love and peace, although every murder committed "for the glory of God" deserves to be condemned in the strongest terms. At least it is well known that in later times, swords have been replaced with medical bags, and instead of cannons, equipment suitable for drilling wells has been used to help spread Christianity.

The idea of keeping Christianity to oneself was not originally an ideal, but what about today? There are still many Christians who are eager to share the gospel with those who have not heard it before, but there are also those of us who are passive and do not recognize a suitable role for ourselves in such activities.

In modern times, especially in Western countries, people have largely adopted a very individualistic attitude towards everything. Faith is one of those things that people prefer to hide from others, but it is not necessarily because they are ashamed to be followers of Jesus.

A partial explanation for the silence may also be that people are too eager to avoid imposing their faith on those who do not want to hear about it. Keeping faith a private matter ensures that no one is subjected to unwanted conversion attempts, but it also means that those interested in Christianity do not get to see the genuine and personal version of Christianity lived out by ordinary people. In this case, the visible manifestation of faith are left to institutions called churches and congregations.

I am sure that every religion, political ideology, or lifestyle is most easily accepted and adopted when one can closely observe someone living as they teach. Greater openness in all matters would make life easier for everyone.

One difficulty in modern times is that everyone suppos-
edly has their own truth that others are not allowed to
disturb. Thus, someone may wait for years for someone
to come along and help solve a personal problem, but no
one comes. Even those who have effective solutions refrain from sharing them, acting in the name of respecting
the individual's freedom of choice.

Unfortunately, our time also has the opposite tendency:
the goal of gaining more members for one's community,
which justifies the community's existence and gives its
leaders a social status in proportion to the number of
members. This mentality may lead to the recruit's interest being secondary to his instrumental value. This reality
is widely known, which tends to close mouths and hearts.
Sometimes a person may feel that the expectations
placed on them become unbearably high if they publicly
identify as a Christian. It is true that Christianity ideally
involves doing good things and avoiding bad ones, but a
person's own goodness is never enough, and he will never
become perfect in this world.

The pursuit of ethical and spiritual superiority alongside
others becomes burdensome for everyone. People should
leave judgment entirely to God so that even those who
feel inadequate dare to confess their faith.

A person may also be so uncertain of his faith that he
does not want to invite others to jump onto the same
shaky bridge. If this is the reason for keeping faith private, I think it is a better solution than forcing a fake

smile and advertising a weak faith as strong just because of social pressure.

I believe that even uncertain faith should be discussed. Genuine searching is at least easier to talk about than ignorance compressed into rigid dogmatism and infallibility. Honesty and authenticity always win over feigned certainty.

Why should I pray?

Jesus' followers asked him to teach them how to pray. The Lord's Prayer was his example of a good prayer. I won't repeat that prayer here, as I believe most people living in a Christian country have heard it at least once, probably many times. Many have likely prayed it repeatedly, following Jesus' example.

The Lord's Prayer focuses on the essentials, starting with addressing God respectfully and asking for God's will to be done everywhere. Only after that are human desires brought forth.

I believe this was the model Jesus urged people to follow in their prayers: Prayers should primarily focus on asking for God's will to be done. This is puzzling because the Almighty surely accomplishes His will even without human requests, and presumably does not leave His will undone even if a small human opposes it.

God is said to love people and want good for us. As the All-Knowing, He is also aware of what we need or imagine we need. Wouldn't one single prayer in childhood suffice then? It could go like this: "God, let Your will be done everywhere and in every moment of my remaining life. Amen."

Then there would be no need to pray ever again. One could freely focus on his own life. Why does something in this thinking feel odd?

I think there are several things out of place. Firstly, it would be unusual for a person to speak to his father or mother only briefly, rarely, and just because it has to be done. If one believes God is the Heavenly Father, he would likely speak to Him quite often. The thought feels natural.

On the other hand, a person's normal life includes various challenges, big and small. Why wouldn't I, as a student, pray for the strength to prepare for exams as well as possible? Why wouldn't I pray to learn everything I need to know to be able to perform my job? Why wouldn't I pray for protection on all my journeys and ask for understanding to make good choices at many crossroads in my life?

Most people with their own children understand the central importance of their children succeeding and coping well with the challenges and adversities of their own lives. I admit that my faith has never been very strong, but I have often felt good about praying for my children.

It may be that God does not need my prayers for anything, but He still likes it when I babble my childish thoughts to Him. As an ordinary father, I at least enjoy listening to what my own children want to tell me.

And in difficult situations, it is healthier for me to pray for help from a higher authority than to just spin worried thoughts in my head. Thoughts have sometimes been called secular prayers that lack a target.

Do prayers then matter for the fulfillment of a person's desires? Do they have any other benefit than calming the mind and focusing on receiving help instead of letting restless and sometimes painful thoughts just scatter everywhere?

Do prayers cause things to happen that wouldn't otherwise? Does God change His mind if a person prays? As a father, I might very well change my mind after discussing

things with my children. Maybe God does so at least sometimes.

Still, it is hard for me to believe that any person could
force or pressure God to do anything. I don't think we
should even try. I believe that when I pray for God's will to
be done, I might change more myself and begin to see
things from a new perspective.

The Bible speaks in many places about persistent prayer
and not giving up too soon if there seems to be no answer
to prayers. Sometimes it even speaks of prayer battles and
the victories achieved through them. I do not oppose or
despise such things. Still, it seems to me that people sometimes have magical beliefs that God could be bent to serve
human interests.

Ultimately, I believe that the greatest impact of prayer
is that a person gets to sit in the lap of the Heavenly Father
and feels so good that he might stop sulking for a moment
when they see a glimpse of a greater purpose than just getting an answer to his own prayers.

Sometimes it seems to me that those who pray aloud in
congregations think more about the people around them
than about God Himself. They cannot simply forget that
others are listening to their prayer evaluatively, so they
choose their words to meet others' expectations or even
tell others about their past week's events through the
words of the prayer.

Jesus said not to imagine that God hears people's prayers because of their many words. Still, it seems to me that
some believers have a habit of stretching their prayers as

long as possible so that at least other believers would give them praise, if not even God Himself.

It may well be that I make things too complicated, but it is easier for me to be genuine when I pray silently in my mind. Praying aloud in front of people tempts me to appear more spiritual than I actually am.

Is it acceptable to be rich?

Jesus once said that it is easier for a camel to go through the eye of a needle than for a rich person to enter the kingdom of God. The Bible contains many other references to rich people whose lives are not exemplary for anyone.

On the other hand, many people who are held up as examples in the Bible were quite wealthy by the standards of their time, and based on their high relative status, they could well be compared to modern billionaires.

So, is wealth a good or bad thing? I suspect that it all depends on the role that wealth plays in a person's life. It is said that once a person's wealth exceeds a certain level, it gradually begins to own the person. This may be a real danger in the lives of some rich people.

If a person's guiding star in life is the pursuit of wealth and they succeed in it, it is very likely that money will continue to have a harmfully central role in his life. A person does not easily change his values once he has achieved a high economic status. It is more likely that he will continue to actively accumulate wealth thereafter.

In the worst case, a rich person may never be satisfied with his wealth and will always want a little more. This need may be based on the fear of the sudden loss of wealth and the security it brings. The pursuit of continuous wealth may also be due to sheer greed.

The fear of sudden poverty and greed are both unpleasant travel companions and may prevent a person from focusing on more important things. A rich person may sometimes neglect even his own family or resort to ethically and legally wrong means in accumulating wealth.

It is clear that poverty does not make a person immune to the temptations of wrongdoing. And it is also true that many very wealthy people have significantly and voluntarily helped those in weaker positions.

Do the rich then have a direct obligation to help the less fortunate, and if so, in what ways? I believe they have a moral and ethical obligation to provide assistance to those in need. And in a sense, they do so by paying taxes, but I do not think the taxation of the rich should be increased to the point where their wealth begins to diminish.

If taxation is so severe that no one can become wealthy, I believe this has a negative impact on people's actions: No one has a personal motive to build productive business if the state immediately takes away the economic benefit of the business.

Excessive taxation of the rich is not essentially a better option than a socialist revolution. Both take away something from people by force that they have acquired through their own work, creativity, and courage.

Some people have the skill to create profitable business and wealth. The political system should allow them to use their skills without punishing them. However, wealth accumulation should not be based on the exploitation of the weaker: The state must prevent such unethical ways of making business profitable.

If business does not rely on the exploitation of the weaker and society allows wealth accumulation through honest means without excessively raising taxes, some people will become wealthy. Only when this happens can we begin to talk about the obligation of the rich to voluntarily help the less fortunate.

The ideal of philanthropy should not be raised so high that the rich should give away their wealth in significant amounts. However, if someone voluntarily gives away some of his wealth, he certainly act honorably.

The core issues are the rich person's obligation to help the less fortunate and that they do so of their own free will. Communism said, "What is yours is mine." Christian love for one's neighbor turns the situation upside down: "What is mine is yours."

In my opinion, a Christian can be very wealthy if the wealth is acquired through honest means. I believe it is not enough to follow the laws set by people, but a Christian should also avoid manipulating others to donate money for purposes that serve more the person's own pursuit of status than anything else.

If a TV pastor who has amassed a fortune appeals to ordinary people's desire to promote the spread of Christianity by asking them to donate funds for a private jet, I believe he is acting wrongly. No person can be so important in God's plans that poorer people should buy him an airplane.

Should we get involved in politics?

God has given humans free will, and people use it. Some for good, others for evil, but fortunately, no one makes only bad decisions, and on the other hand, no one can completely avoid wrong choices.

When God Himself has given people the freedom to choose how they live, no human has the right or duty to restrict this freedom unless it causes concrete harm to other people.

If an individual's actions cause serious consequences for others, people have the right and duty to set boundaries on what is permissible and what is forbidden. If people allowed all actions, it would no longer be an organized society, but we could talk about anarchy.

It is not self-evident which actions and their consequences are so problematic that society must strive to prevent them. People are known to have many different opinions, and the democratic process must be able to produce laws that bind all citizens despite this.

Christians are sometimes concerned about changes in customs and culture, as are most other people. Everyone has the right to advocate for laws that best ensure the realization of their own values in society.

Against this background, it is natural that some Christians seek to influence legislation through political activity. This is entirely acceptable in a democracy. If a person represents a small minority in his values, it is unlikely that his thoughts will significantly influence the laws enacted. Still, a Christian has the same right as others to try to influence decisions.

No citizen representing a minority should be surprised if many laws enacted by the majority are poor in his opinion. Christian politicians are no exception: In a democracy, everyone must be prepared for the fact that no minority can demand the majority to live according to the minority's terms.

Christians often cannot force non-Christians to live according to Christian values through legislation, nor can they always achieve legislation that allows Christians to live according to their own values.

In political rhetoric, however, there is sometimes an attempt to silence the promotion of Christian values by appealing to the idea that religion and politics should not be mixed. Such a claim is colored by a certain political ideology. One could equally well say that no ideology should be promoted in politics or that politics should not operate according to different opinions and values, which would be nonsense.

People have the right to make an ideological statement that Christianity should not be considered when enacting laws, but this too is just an opinion. There is no neutral and universally shared value other than everyone's right to advocate for things important to him.

Another way to try to silence those who make Christian politics is to refer to the idea that the state should not interfere with people's freedom to decide for themselves. This is a nonsensical demand, as the state's specific task is to ensure that individuals' actions are sufficiently in harmony with the interests of the entire society.

Reconciling the different aspirations of individuals and society requires that everyone has the right to express his own opinions. The entire democracy is based on this. After open discussion, a vote is held, and the majority's view wins.

When lawmakers have reached a decision on a political issue, it binds everyone, even if it means using one's own tax funds for purposes that the citizen himself does not accept based on his own values.

I have heard some politicians advocate the idea that lawmakers should at least discuss the need to limit parents' ability to raise their children. Such thoughts do not represent a neutral and objective value system, even if they may try to present their demands in such a light.

For example, if an atheist minister suggests that minors should not be exposed to religious upbringing at home, this is not a neutral stance but an attempt to restrict individual freedoms. Such restriction is justified only if it is indisputable that the child's well-being is in real danger. That the religious values adopted by the child could be harmful to the child, in the atheist politician's thinking, is not sufficient evidence.

Equally well, a Christian politician could demand that atheism should not be taught at home. Such demands extending into homes are absurd, and it would be impossible to monitor compliance with laws enacted based on them.

Parents naturally and unintentionally pass on their thought patterns to their children. The child has later the freedom to reject or accept the ideological heritage of his home. This is as natural as learning the language or languages spoken at home. No one suggests that a child should not be spoken to in any minority language until he reaches adulthood, after which he could decide whether he wants to adopt the language spoken by his parents.

The right to express different views belongs to democracy, and Christian politicians also have the right to promote their views, even if the majority of citizens do not share their values. Restricting political activity and freedom of speech is against democracy.

Amazing Grace

No one can ever live perfectly according to any ideals. Therefore, Christians have a superior product to offer: Grace.

Grace means God's unmerited love and favor for humanity. And if my imperfections and wickedness are forgiven, I am also expected to treat others with grace.

To create an acronym, the word GRACE could also be said to be formed from the initial letters of the words: God's Radical Acceptance Covers Everyone.

Treating others with grace does not mean that I or anyone else has the right to do whatever comes to mind, whether good or bad. As a Christian, I must always avoid evil and strive to do good.

I understand that grace is like a tow truck that takes a broken-down vehicle to the repair shop for free. It is like an ambulance that takes a person to the hospital when needed.

However, grace does not automatically take a person wherever they happen to want to go. Grace is not a white limousine that transports a man to a gentlemen's club striptease show or a cocaine party.

Repentance is an essential part of receiving grace. If a person does not feel he has done wrong, they do not seek grace either.

Many people want to make the conditions for receiving grace stricter than God Himself, from whom the whole concept originates. If someone has filed a fraudulent tax return but repents and corrects the matter, most are likely ready to let grace prevail over justice. If a man cheats on his wife but repents and asks for forgiveness from his wife and God, some may make the justification for grace dependent on the wife's ability and willingness to forgive her husband.

If a person repeatedly commits the same condemnable act but repents every single time, how many times does he deserve grace? The answer is that he does not deserve grace at all, for grace cannot be earned. God forgives them endlessly if they repent and ask God to be gracious.

But what if a person has committed murder and can no longer ask for forgiveness from his victim? Is it right for God to still be gracious?

And if we go further down the scale of evil, can someone who repents of child abuse be forgiven by God, even if no human could forgive them?

What about Stalin or Hitler, who were responsible for the deaths of millions of people? If they had repented, would God have forgiven them too?

My understanding is that grace is sufficient in all cases, but not everyone feels they need it, no matter how horrific their actions. Evil deeds may have changed a person so much that he can no longer repent and see himself as guilty. If a person defends himself or blames others for his actions, I do not believe he is ready to receive God's grace.

But can it be just for someone to escape the consequences of his actions by appealing to grace, no matter how horrific his deeds?

Firstly, he cannot escape the consequences of his actions in this life but may, for example, end up in prison to atone for his deeds according to human laws. Additionally, he is likely to be mentally crippled for the rest of his life. He does not escape the consequences of their actions in this life.

However, God's grace is a reality regardless of how difficult or easy it is for others to forgive the repentant.

Jesus made it clear that people have no right to judge anyone or withhold forgiveness. The reason is that every person has sinned and needs grace. A person will be left without grace himself if he does not show it to others.